I'm a

R♡mance Scam

IT Detective

A True Story

Selina Co

Publisher: Inspiring Publishers,
P.O. Box 159, Calwell, ACT Australia 2905
Email: publishaspg@gmail.com
http://www.inspiringpublishers.com

 A catalogue record for this
book is available from the
NATIONAL
LIBRARY   National Library of Australia
OF AUSTRALIA

National Library of Australia The Prepublication Data Service

Front cover design by Selina Co
Artworks and hand-drawn icons by Selina Co

Author: Selina Co
Title: I'm a Romance Scam IT Detective
Genre: True Crime / Family & Relationships / Psychological Thriller
ISBN: 978-1-922327-16-1 (Edition 2)

Photo A: Frederick's photo on his (fake) engineering company website. (Refer to P.16 & 43) Looked like he was really an engineer?

Photo B (suppressed): Frederick claimed he also built bridges. (Refer to P. 16)

< Frederick wearing a suit. The background was a construction site for building a bridge across the sea. >

Nothing suspicious.

Photo C (suppressed): Frederick claimed to be outside his office. (Refer to P. 24)

< Frederick in a long-sleeved, blue work shirt. He was relaxing on an outdoor sofa, holding a glass of red wine.>

Selina thought, 'Vineyard? The venue looks like a vineyard.' She examined the background of the photo but there was no obvious vineyard structure to prove it.

Later (Refer to P. 64), Selina pointed out that the background of this photo did not match his office address. Then Frederick changed his story, saying he was in a conference meeting in this photo.

Photo D (suppressed): Frederick said he gave a speech at a conference.

(Refer to P. 23)

There was a big, golden sign in the venue. Selina magnified it to check whether it has any mismatch to his story. However, the words remained unclear after magnifying due to low resolution.

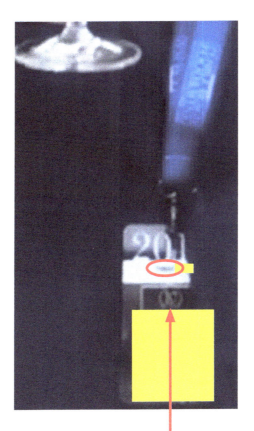

Video 1 (suppressed): Frederick holding a glass of champagne. Cheers to you and me! (Refer to P. 23)

He has a name tag in the video. Selina magnified it to see if it matched his name "Frederick Chong". However, after magnifying, resolution was still not high enough to see the name tag. "Frxxxxx"? It seemed too short for "Frederick", but this was not certain.

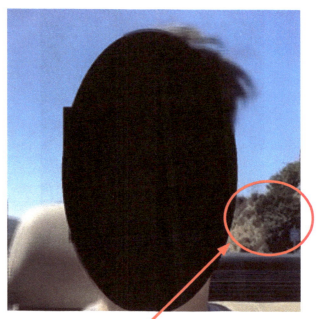

Video 2: (Refer to P. 72) Frederick claimed to be driving from Brooklyn to New York CBD. Selina said, 'California … Los Angeles?'

No one will normally post a video of driving and smiling in front of camera on Facebook or social media. He must have sent this out himself.

The way he smiled was like he was smiling at his lover. But was it me?

Photo E: Frederick's fake US passport (Refer to P. 68)—he didn't smile and looked directly at the camera. It really looked like a real passport photo.

And it did have some patterns on it, like a usual passport.

Photo F: <Above, left> Embarrassed smile when taking photos with her best friends at her so-called "wedding". (Refer to P. 35)

Everyone else in the photo was smiling happier than her.

Contrast to her always very big, wooden smile whenever the alleged target came by.

The above was a rare photo that this extraordinary bride celebrated her "big day" with best friends. Half of displayed wedding day photos were her best friends celebrating ... without her!

If humans tend to express true feelings in front of best friends, then can you tell how she thinks about this "marriage"?

By the way, why did she rush into this "marriage" in a hurry?

<Below> She always smiles the same big, wooden smile, no matter her posture or the situation (except when her best friends celebrated her "wedding").

But it is not a happy nor excited smile either—try yourself with a mirror. You need an effort to post such very big, plastic smile. The unnatural big smile often fails to match her posture.

Women in love never behave like this. The actress needs to improve her acting.

CHASE ⬡

Consumer International Wire Transfer Combined Disclosure and Receipt

JPMorgan Chase Bank, N.A.
270 Park Avenue, Manhattan,
New York, NY 10017, United States

Today's Date: 5/21/2018
Wire Transfer Date: 5/21/2018

Date Funds Available to Recipient: 5/25/2018
Chase Wire Tracking Number: JF1JZZ1U00KP

SENDER:
FEDERICK CHONG
77 WATER ST, NYC
NEW YORK 10005
USA

RECIPIENT:
(Selina's passport name)

RECIPIENT BANK:
Selina's bank name,
bank address
Selina's bank account #)

CTBAAU2S

Exchange Rate: $1 USD = 1 USD

Amount to be Deducted from Your Account:		Amount to be Received by the Recipient:		
Transfer Amount:	$113,000.00	Transfer Amount:	113,000.00	USD
Transfer Fees:	+$50.00	Other Fees:*	-0.00	USD
Transfer Taxes:	+$0.00			
Total:	$113,050.00	Total to Recipient	113,000.00	USD
		*charged by other institutions		

The recipient may receive less due to fees charged by the recipient's bank and foreign taxes.

If you provided us an incorrect account number for the Recipient or an incorrect routing or identification number for the Recipient's bank, you could lose the amount of the transfer.

You have a right to dispute errors in your transaction. If you think there is an error, contact us within 180 days at 1-888-434-3030 or send an account inquiry via Secure Message Center on chase.com. You can also contact us for a written explanation of your rights.

You can cancel this wire transfer at no cost within 30 minutes after you have authorized us to send this wire transfer. Please contact 1-800-935-9935 or visit a Chase branch.

If you have question or complaints about JPMorgan Chase Bank, N.A. contact:
Consumer Financial Protection Bureau
1-855-411-2372
1-855-729-2372 (TTY/TDD)
www.consumerfinance.gov

M1211-13-CS WPDP (13/16)

Photo G: JP Morgan Chase banking document stating that Frederick had already transferred USD 113,000 to Selina. JP Morgan Chase in New York refused to comment on whether this banking document was real or fake and whether this customer existed or not, due to privacy reasons. (Refer to P. 68)

(It is not to criticise on whether banks are right or wrong to do so.)

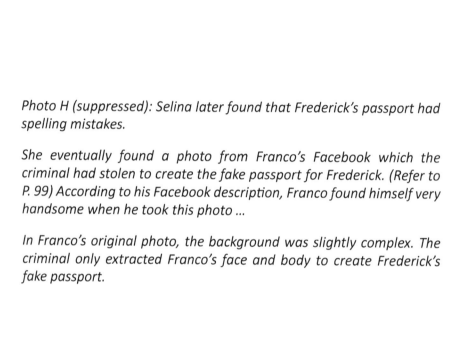

Photo H (suppressed): Selina later found that Frederick's passport had spelling mistakes.

She eventually found a photo from Franco's Facebook which the criminal had stolen to create the fake passport for Frederick. (Refer to P. 99) According to his Facebook description, Franco found himself very handsome when he took this photo ...

In Franco's original photo, the background was slightly complex. The criminal only extracted Franco's face and body to create Frederick's fake passport.

Disclaimer

This book is based on a 95% real story. People's names, countries, places and dates are intentionally altered (scammer's fake name Frederick Chong was the actual fake name he used). Irrelevant personal attributes were slightly altered to protect the identities of Selina, Jason, Franco and other innocent people in this book.

This book is accurate enough for your understanding on Internet scams and romance scams, but not accurate enough to solicit against any character in this novel (except against Frederick Chong).

We are documenting what happened as accurately as we can, which has involved a number of government agencies. We support and appreciate almost all of these government agencies. The purpose in documenting these is to express what can be done better. We hope to contribute to a better world, instead of blaming any of the organizations involved.

Further, while the story involves Australia, Singapore and the United States, this book is not intended to comment on nor to criticise any particular country's policies, but uses these only as a solid example of what can happen in a romance scam.

Contents

MEETING FREDERICK

Basketball or dinner?

Selina: I don't remember I am 38. My clients say I look 20 and surprisingly boys aged 19 or 20 still want to date me as they say I look young and pretty. I never expected that I, as an IT consultant, would fall victim to an Internet romance scam, losing 70% of my life savings.

And … I didn't know I could become so dangerous …

On 4 May 2018, I was on a flight back from my home town Macau to Australia, my home. New start. Lost support from a few friends recently. What were the new things ahead of me?

The next day, Monday, was a usual working day—but not so usual. 'Lady, your access card has expired again,' security said. The client had forgotten to extend my consultancy access to their office—it occasionally happens, and implies I need to work from home for a few days, until they sort things out.

'Singapore team, how are things going?' I asked.

'Selina, welcome back. We have few issues that we are working on. These are in our area so you can relax for the day. We'll ping you when we need you.'

'Okay,' I said.

Sitting in my home, getting to my big balcony.

Relaxing day … Boring day … Okay, empty day.

He's not good-looking

In the afternoon, Selina received a message from a guy called Frederick Chong through her Meetup.com apps.

'Hi here, I am Frederick from New York, Manhattan area. I am a civil engineer,' Frederick said.

(Meetup.com is an online platform for people in the same city with similar interests or purposes to sign up to events to do something together in person. They have social events, sports, business gatherings, or just a coffee in a lazy afternoon. It is useful for new immigrants like Selina who have been in Australia for only six years to meet more friends and get support from neighbours. Tourists visiting the city may also sign up to meet new local friends at their gatherings. *Meetup* is where Selina groups herself with new friends to play basketball, have dinner, go camping, etc.

Meetup.com has groups in most countries and cities such as Brisbane, Seoul, Sydney, Macau, New York, Hong Kong, Singapore, Ghana, Peru, Los Angeles, Tokyo …)

Frederick was not very good-looking, with lots of moles on his face. In Selina's opinion, having many moles was a sign of bad health. But the word "civil engineer" did catch Selina's attention, as it made her think of Jason. And after all, he did not look too awful. She replied, 'Hi.'

Selina looked into his Meetup.com profile. This Frederick was from San Jose, California, according to his profile, and he was interested in making friends across Australia, Taiwan, Malaysia and Singapore. Selina guessed that he must have travelled to those countries before, and when he went there, he joined Meetup.com to meet with local people for a drink or a coffee. It is quite usual for Western travellers to do so, as it helps to understand local culture, get good recommendations from the locals and make travel more fun and meaningful.

Many things on the Internet are not real, especially people and websites. Selina was careful. She examined his Whatsapp phone number—it was from Georgia? How come a San Jose person currently living in Manhattan registered his phone in Georgia? Furthermore, not many people live in Manhattan. It's not a residential area. Selina wanted to challenge him, but couldn't think of how to. So, she just directly asked him all these, and he just said these were all true.

Selina said, 'What a coincidence. I have a lot of relatives in Georgia, though we are not close as they rarely come back to China. Indeed, I myself previously had US residence but our family decided not to go.'

'I am an independent civil engineer. I mainly work on civil engineering works on oil rig structures. I have my own office and a few employees in New York. I have been to many countries, including all Asian countries, Turkey and France. My parents were from Macau, and I was born in New York.'

'I am an IT consultant in financial systems. My work is mainly to explain to business how to use our systems, so my work is not so technical at the moment, but I used to be a technical person … I have been to 20 countries in my life, and went to New York and Los Angeles just last year. I don't love travelling, but I happen to travel a lot in my life … You've been to all Asian countries? That's a lot! I'm from Macau … And, you know what? I used to work in the construction industry as well.'

'That's brilliant! I work on civil engineering works in oil rigs and pipelines. My work is very complex.' And Frederick showed her a photo where he was wearing a safety hat *(photo A)* in the field. And another photo *(photo B)*, where he was next to a road construction area near the sea.

So maybe he really was an engineer. But was he really the person in the photos? And was he telling her the truth about his background?

Not supposed to be online dating

As mentioned, Meetup.com is mainly for gathering real people to meet face-to-face. In other words, Selina did not actually realize it was online dating, and she was not prepared for it. Selina was under an impression that Frederick was a visitor currently in Sydney. However, Frederick explained that he was currently in New York, preparing to travel to New Zealand for work soon. He expected to visit an old friend in Sydney when he came to the region. When he was looking for his friend's contact in Meetup.com, he came across Selina's photo and was impressed by Selina's beauty.

Selina was not actually looking for anyone. She was not especially interested in talking to Frederick, but she barely had any work to do those few days while everything was waiting for her colleagues. So, Frederick and Selina talked day and night for three days, except when Frederick went to work. By the fourth day since they had known each other, Frederick said, 'Selina, there is something I want to talk to you about … I am so shy …'

'Tell me.'

'Dear, I have been thinking seriously about you and I, I know we've just met but I have strong feelings for you. Let me use the word LOVE because I find my heart so close to you now and hope you'll give me a chance in your heart. I know we are far apart but I can promise you that distance is not going to be a problem because I am used to travelling a lot because of the nature of my job. All I am asking for is just a little space in your heart. When I come to New Zealand, I'll have a woman that I can call my love and someone I can hold on to. Please let me know what you think about this.'

Selina was not surprised. After all, she was still quite attractive—at least, that was what people told her. 'I am happy to hear that. How long will you stay in New Zealand this time? ☺,' she replied.

'Three to four months.'

'That's great! ☺.'

'Dear, I developed feelings fast for you.'

'☺.'

'All I mostly need from you is to love me, and marry me if you feel something for me.'

'Ok. We will meet and see how we feel.'

'Thanks, dear … My heart is full of joy.'

Now, Selina was a bit amazed, but not very. To be honest, boys' words do not always reflect what they actually think. Just recently, she'd met a guy who'd said he wanted to marry her when they first talked. When they met another time, he said he wanted to be her boyfriend. After meeting a few times, he said he only wanted to be no strings attached.

Sometimes, when a boy says 'I want to marry you!', it just means, 'I am interested in you a bit.' (Sorry, I hope I have not offended all boys. I'm only talking about "some" boys.)

Frederick continued, 'I'll be working in New Zealand. I'm happy to pay for your flight to meet with me in New Zealand.'

It wasn't much money. But why not? Selina said, 'That sounds good.'

Google search

From the first day Selina had met this Frederick Chong, she'd been searching for his information online. But there was no Frederick Chong on the Internet that matched his background. "Chong" is a common surname in the Canton area (Macau, Hong Kong, Guangzhou, etc), so that made sense. According to Google, "Chong" can also be an African surname.

Anyway, there was no information found about this "Frederick Chong", at least none from the United States with his face. In this modern world, almost everyone has a Facebook or LinkedIn or something on the web. Frederick Chong had nothing. That was strange.

Unusual English accent: a red flag or his deficiency?

Soon, Selina attempted to call him, as she thought he had attempted to call her. Wah! His voice was terrible! Super throaty! And the sound of his speaking voice … it was like an Indian! She hated it! It didn't mean she hated Indians, but someone who looked Chinese, born and grew up in the United States should not have an Indian voice—it just didn't match. As Selina is a musician, she loves beautiful voices and she really hates hearing a voice like his—horribly throaty, weird accent. Such terrible throatiness like this can be due to i) growing up in poor conditions, or ii) born to have a terrible voice. In contrast, the man Selina loves, Jason, his voice is very attractive to her. Jason does not sing well, but his speaking voice is firm with medium strength, and his pitch is just perfect.

Coming back to Frederick, Selina said to him, 'Your voice is really terrible.'

You would almost describe it as a deficiency. His voice sounded like a devil—it just had a horrible, terrible quality! But sometimes you just need to accept people. Everyone has good and bad bits. In some people's eyes, this bad point would not matter at all. To Selina, voice quality is important because she is a musician … but indeed, it is unimportant to life. So, she thought she'd better accept it.

'You said you grew up in New York. How come you don't have an American accent?'

'Yes, my accent is close to my parents', Frederick replied.

< Selina thought: It is not a Macau accent either. Maybe people in the olden days had a different accent? >

Selina texted her close friend Anna in Melbourne, who grew up in Australia. Anna texted her back, 'Usually, if someone grew up in an English-speaking country, their accent should be native.' Selina was disappointed: that meant Frederick must be a fake.

Anna paused and continued, 'Oh yes, I did encounter one case. A guy's English really sounded like his parents' because they had a very close relationship and he didn't like to socialise with other people. This is an exception.'

Okay, so Frederick was this type of exception. He said he had a very close relationship with his parents when they were alive.

Another interesting thing: Frederick's parents were from Macau, but he himself could not understand Chinese at all. He said it was because his parents wanted him to be very American, so they intentionally didn't teach him Chinese.

Okay, so it must be that his parents only spoke English to him, but his parents' English wasn't good. So, he picked up the wrong English accent and wrong English grammar from his parents (his English only had minor problems). If he was an introvert and didn't like making friends and he only had a close relationship with his parents, this might be possible, though unlikely.

Anyway, these were his deficiencies in Selina's eyes.

Consistent care and concern

'Honey, I close my eyes and I can see you clearly. I open my eyes and I can see your mighty love ... You really are my own love,' said Frederick.

He continued, 'I feel so loved when you say something sweet to me. Even a whisper from your sweet lips can make me have a really wonderful day. You are the one I see in my dreams and **I'm glad you are a reality**. Good morning, my love.'

Selina knew some of this was copied from classical poems—who cares? A previous guy in Beijing, he also sent her classical poems. Some boys think it's romantic, or they simply don't know what to say.

Now, every morning (Frederick's night time in the US), he talked to Selina.

'So, how long does it take for you to travel to work?' asked Frederick.

'I usually take public transport, and then the company bus—in total, one hour.'

'Okay. You need to be careful.'

'Careful of what?'

'You need to be careful of the pressure from work.'

< *Selina thought: This seems strange. A top engineer like him, why is he so concerned about pressure from work? I just go to work. I've never said there is a lot of pressure or overtime, nor that the work is difficult.* >

'Sure. Love you!' Selina replied.

'Remember to take your breakfast.' Frederick said this every day.

'Don't worry. Breakfast is my favourite meal. I skip lunch but never breakfast … By the way, do you know there is a *"Breakfast Political Party"* in Hong Kong?'

'No, I don't.'

'Because they always have meetings at breakfast, so they take the call.'

'Haha, honey, you are funny.'

Playing hockey together

'My love, what are you doing?'

'Frederick, good morning to you (and good evening to myself). I'm playing hockey tonight.'

'You know what? I don't want you to play hockey. I don't want you to get injured.'

'But I really love it. I'm healthier since I started playing hockey. It's obvious.'

'Okay, as long as you love it. Can you take a photo when you are there? I want to be with you.'

'Sure.'

So, Selina took a photo of the hockey field and showed him.

'When I come to Australia, show me your skills.'

'Haha, I have no skills. I'm only playing for fun. But sure, we can play together.'

Solid plans to meet

'Have you heard about a place called Awakino?'

Selina searched from the web. 'Yes—Awakino in New Zealand.'

'That's where I will be working. On week days, I'll work there. On weekends, I'll meet you in Auckland. Expenses will be covered by my contract.'

'Great. It's 3.5 hours' drive to Auckland.'

There was an airport in New Plymouth, close to Awakino. He could take a flight on Friday night to Auckland, and return on Sunday evening. It would be only an hour's flight. This kind of fly-in fly-out package was common in Australia's mining industry. On weekdays, workers and professionals stay in remote parts of Australia. On weekends, they fly back to their family in towns like Melbourne, Perth and Sydney. Alternatively, they stay in remote areas for weeks at a time, then return to their families in town for one or two weeks.

'I've been to Auckland twice. Have you ever been there?' asked Frederick.

'No, not yet. I previously got temporary residence in New Zealand, but decided not to even land.'

'Good. I'll take you around.'

14 photos and two personal videos

Selina examined each of his photos, magnifying them to see if anything failed to match what he'd said.

Like the above photo in his "company speech" (photo D), there was a big golden sign behind him. Selina magnified it to see if any words on the sign contradicted what he'd said. For example, he'd said he was an engineer, would the sign say it was an accounting association? But the words were not clear enough for her to examine.

In his personal video (video 1), he was wearing a name tag. Due to low resolution, after magnifying, Selina could only see "Frxxxxx" and not his detailed name. Really, the name looked a little bit shorter than "Frederick", but at least the "Frxxxxx" seemed to match.

There was another photo where he claimed to be outside his office (*photo C*). Selina thought, 'Vineyard … the background looks like a vineyard.' (Selina loved vineyards.) But she didn't find any obvious vineyard structures to prove it. 'Could it be my mistake? Maybe it's just a garden? Or maybe his office is next to a vineyard? Possibly he lives in Manhattan, and his office is in a remote area.'

Selina also checked his hair length and hair style against the timeline, as some of the photos were claimed to be taken "today". But boys' hair is usually short, and it was hard to find anything obviously wrong.

No contradiction was found.

Why had government warnings failed?

So, it happened to be the Australian government's "Scam Awareness Week" when she met Frederick …

At that time, Selina wasn't aware that it was a "Scam Awareness Week". She only noticed this more than half a year later when she read the old news. Why? In the "Scam Awareness Week", Selina only saw one single advertisement on TV about all types of scams. The advertisements had only spent a few seconds on romance scams, showing a cartoon dragon sitting behind a computer doing something very colourful (like playing fireworks?) while chatting online with a girl. No details, no statistics, no volumes, no scammers' tricks or techniques were given. It also failed to mention that many people are losing their life savings and going bankrupt.

Selina thought, 'What does this advertisement mean? But one thing is certain: there cannot possibly be a cartoon dragon playing fireworks in front of a computer.' After all, it was the first time in her life she'd seen an advertisement in Australia about scams … The word S-C-A-M was new vocabulary to Selina, a non-native English speaker. She only checked out vocabulary in the dictionary if she frequently saw a word. She understood 'F-R-A-U-D' and 'F-A-

K-E' and 'I-L-L-E-G-I-T-I-M-A-T-E'. She'd studied English since pre-school when she was two, but for some reason, this elegant word S-C-A-M was new to her.

She thought, 'HAHAHAHA! How would those people possibly send money to someone he or she had only met online? That is crazy. Those victims must be obsessed. It will surely not happen to me.'

'It must be a rare problem,' she thought. 'Otherwise, why would there be no TV news and barely any government advertisements? TV news in Australia only tell you how global warming's going or how birds are playing in front of cinemas.'

There were three TV advertisements per day telling you to save water; but for scams, Selina only saw one single TV ad in Australia in her whole life, which covered all types of scams within 30 seconds.

'It could not possibly happen to me,' Selina thought. 'First, Jason is the only love of my life. Frederick could only be a substitute if Jason really doesn't come back. Second, I am very careful and will check everything.'

She thought further, 'Maybe this Frederick is fake? But what's the problem? He promises he is going to meet me in New Zealand soon. Worse case, I walk away if I don't like him when I meet him in person. No harm.'

STATISTICS

According to Australian Scamwatch figures, each year, almost 4,000 Australians are reported to be victimised in romance scams. This accounts for losses of more than AUD 20 million—this is only the official figure. It is estimated that 70–90% of romance scams are unreported to police or government, possibly due to embarrassment.

According to the FBI's Internet Crime Complaint Center (IC3), 18,493 complaints were categorised as confidence fraud or romance scams, with financial losses exceeding USD 362.5 million in 2018 alone. According to the news, many victims lose their life savings, some become bankrupted and are forced to sell their homes to cover the monetary losses.

It is also known that Internet romance scams are targeted at countries including Australia, New Zealand, the United Kingdom, the United States, Canada, Hong Kong, Singapore, Israel, Japan, and Korea.

Most victims are well educated, including professors, successful business people and IT consultants …

But why are so many well-educated people losing their life savings to these Internet scams? What is the magic? Is the word "L-O-V-E" the answer to everything? You will understand, after reading this book. You can also check out our latest analysis and romance scammers' latest known tricks at our company website:

https://www.onlinedatingidentitycheck.com.au

UNFORTUNATE
COINCIDENCES

Many people believe unusual coincidences are signs of God's will. Unfortunately, in reality, only God's will is God's will; coincidences are just coincidences.

Dinner and breakfast

To draw Selina further into this "relationship", Frederick asked her to have lunch or dinner "together" (at the same time, but of course, in a different location). They would exchange pictures of the food they were eating.

'I made my breakfast today,' said Frederick, and sent her a picture of a Chinese roll, with a paper cup of coffee.

Selina examined the picture. That was crazy! As a master chef herself, she could tell this Chinese roll was troublesome to make. It involved a lot of cutting and different cooking methods in a single dish. As a professional civil engineer, why would you bother to make such a complex breakfast yourself on a working day? Selina would only make complex dishes like this in the evening or on weekends.

And look at the table. This wooden table was not like a table in a home. It seemed to be in a hawker centre or a local restaurant. But … Yes, it was possible that someone would put such a table in their home if they had a semi-outdoor area. But the coffee … Why would you use a paper cup at home?

Another challenge was, this dish required a few fresh ingredients and if you were living alone, as Frederick claimed, the remaining ingredients would become un-fresh in one or two days.

Indeed, she remembered that New York was a bit strange. She'd stayed at the Holiday Inn in Manhattan, and the hotel rooms had indeed only paper cups.

'I've seen this Chinese roll before but never eaten it myself. What's the name of this dish? Is it a Cantonese dish?'

(Probably Frederick also didn't know, so he avoided answering this question and pretended to be offline for a while. When he came back, he switched to another topic.)

At night on the same day, Selina went to the city for dinner on her own. She ordered something off the menu in a Beijing-style restaurant … Guess what? That same Chinese roll was delivered to her!

'Frederick, what a surprise! I've got the same dish as what you sent me this morning! It's the first time I've had it.'

'Do you like it?'

'Ah, yes … I'm just surprised.'

Music

Selina still didn't believe that Frederick really meant to marry her, as she thought boys sometimes don't really mean what they say.

Frederick sent Selina a piece of music every day. She didn't always listen to them, because the recent pieces were not very beautiful—not her style. Today, she happened to have some spare time, didn't know what to do, so she listened to "What are words" by Chris Medina that Frederick sent her.

The lyrics were about keeping promises. This music was awesome. Only when she heard that did she realise Frederick was saying what he meant—he really meant to marry her!

Replacement

Selina was excited but worried. She didn't want Frederick to be disappointed.

'Actually, we haven't met yet. Maybe you won't like me when you meet me? Or maybe I won't like you when we meet?' Selina was mainly concerned about the latter.

Frederick said, 'I love you as you are.'

Poor Frederick. According to him, he used to have a girlfriend who died a few years ago when they were about to get married. Since then, he'd felt very sad and hadn't found someone who could replace her in his heart. He added that his girlfriend didn't like sex, so they only had it five times over many years as he respected her. As for his parents, his father was a politician in Los Angeles, and his mother was a medical doctor. Both died in the same motor accident a few years ago. There were too many people around him who had died—it was a bit weird. But this can happen in real life.

< Selina thought: Frederick loves me as I am? Then it is a deep love and it shows he has a good character. Maybe I should treasure it.

Selina thought: Why does he want to marry me within days of meeting? I must have something similar to his parents in heaven or his dead girlfriend. I was also from Macau, so probably we had similar cultural backgrounds, or maybe my face looks like hers. I don't want to ask, I don't want to know. I don't want to know that I am just a replacement. Just like I don't want to tell Frederick that he is only a replacement for Jason. >

Jason and Selina

The Chinese lunar calendar is based on the movement of the moon; the Chinese Moon Festival (Mid-Autumn Festival) is the date with brightest full moon of the year. Candles and colourful lanterns are lit up everywhere to praise the beauty of the full moon. The full moon in the sky is a parable about the union of families and lovers. The Chinese say about the Chinese Moon Festival, "Full moon, family union."

Back in 2011, sole-tourist Selina from Macau had visited Byron Bay for three weeks, preparing to leave. On the afternoon of the Chinese Moon Festival, curious, clumsy Selina walked too fast and crashed straight into Jason! She was about to fall into his chest, so he immediately held her with both of his arms. Selina was astonished! Embarrassed, she slowly lifted her head to look up, and saw Jason smiling gently, looking down at her. They froze for a few seconds. Only then did Selina notice he was such a sweet guy.

The next day, Selina left Byron Bay and continued her adventures in Melbourne before heading back to Macau.

One year later, Selina was granted a permanent skilled migration visa to Australia. When she landed Byron Bay, it was again the yearly Chinese Moon Festival. She looked around to see if there was anyone she could recognise. When Selina walked to the same spot where she crashed into Jason, Jason was right in front of her again.

But they didn't talk until a month later. 'Soo Mao!' Someone called Selina's Chinese name. Who called her? These days, only Selina's family would call her Chinese name. It was Jason! He was talking about a girl, and mentioned a rare vocabulary that has the same pronunciation as Selina's Chinese name. Hearing her name, Selina went over to have a short chat with Jason for the first time.

That night, a dream came upon Selina: Jason was holding a big, red rose, and walking from the left to her front. He got down on one knee, like a marriage proposal, and said, 'Selina, I love you very much. Be my girlfriend, please.'

Everyone around them applauded and shouted, 'Hooray!'

But Selina thought, 'I don't even know you.' She wanted to refuse him. But everyone was there! And ... he looked so sincere. She had a thought, and said, 'We can be friends. We'll decide about us later.' Suddenly, she woke up.

Soon, they became good friends. Jason was a clever, simple-hearted and sincere man. And he always said funny things when he didn't mean to be funny. Selina and Jason could always have a laugh, no matter how tough life was.

Jason and Selina were both engineers. They both loved animals, both used to have a cat in China, both loved the beach, loved baths and loved the Chinese Moon festival. Jason and Selina both loved roses.

Sometimes, when Selina looked in the mirror, she thought Jason walked by. Sometimes, when she looked at Jason's photo, she thought it was herself!

Jason and Selina had always only been good friends.

Selina prayed to God many times, asking 'My Lord, is Jason the man I'm going to marry?'

'Yes,' a voice spoke.

'My Lord, really? Are you sure?'

'Yes,' the voice spoke.

Under the teaching of general charismatic churches, if one humbly praises the Lord and puts God as the most important in his or her life, occasionally a distinct voice from the Holy Spirit would speak to him or her. One obvious sign of this is that the words of the voice have no rational justification, but always yield. This method was frequently used in the Bible (Joshua 9:14, 1 Samuel 23:2, 4, 10-11, Acts 1:24-26).

However, the method has been widely abused. Terrible Christians take whatever they desire or whatever they calculate rationally, and justify this by saying, 'The Holy Spirit says.' To avoid this abuse, typical Christians nowadays would rather argue that there is no such method—but this is wrong. Some pastors and a few general Christians can tell the future using this method accurately; horrifyingly accurately.

Since Selina was 21, she had occasionally heard a voice talking to her when she prayed to God. The words had no rational justification, but always yielded. Therefore, she believed that the Holy Spirit occasionally talked to her in her prayers. She also believed it was the Holy Spirit who had been telling her for years that Jason was the man she was going to marry.

As an IT consultant, Selina had encountered many men in the past 10 years, and she had asked the same question for a number of them: 'Is this man the one I'm going to marry?' The spirit always said, 'No.' She would ask three times and when the voice consistently said, 'No', she wouldn't ask again. Only when Jason walked by did the spirit keep saying, 'Yes.' 'Yes.' 'Sure.' 'Yes, it is certain.'

The Bible also talks a lot about God revealing his will through dreams *(Matthew 1:20-24, Daniel 2:27-28, Matthew 2:2)*. Selina believes in the many dreams that came upon her in regard to Jason.

Anyway, this book is not a religious book. You do not need to agree with or argue against this religious theory. But we must talk about Selina's religious beliefs, because these fully explain why Selina had never actually fallen in love with Frederick.

One day Jason was in Selina's home, helping her with a serious task. While they were talking, suddenly, a voice, possibly from the Holy Spirit, said to Selina, 'You said something that you shouldn't. Therefore, you will not see Jason for three to nine years. This will happen in three months' time, from July 2013.'

And it did happen. She did not see Jason for the next few years.

Selina was worried. Would Jason never come back? She prayed, many times, 'God, Father in heaven, is Jason still to be with me one day? If yes, please let me dream of him and see his face tonight, and not tomorrow.' And the enquiry always received a positive response. (This method to enquire God for His will was used in *Judges 6:36-40*.)

So, she continued to wait for Jason.

Selina prayed to God and asked, 'You said Jason would be my husband, but when will it happen? Is it this year?' The spirit said, 'No.' 'Next year?' 'No.' 'The next year?' 'No.' Selina feared to ask further …

Three years later, on Boxing Day 2015, when Selina prayed and praised God, a voice said, 'Jason is now with another girl, go talk to him immediately. Do not delay.' But Selina didn't know what to say and how to say it. She waited for three months, until Easter, before deciding to talk to Jason to stop him. But she was too late, Jason had already decided. 'I also have a lot of "coincidences" with her, not only with you,' he said.

Selina said, 'I'm not talking about coincidences, I'm talking about enquiring God.'

Jason said, 'What???'

They talked for a while, but Selina was nervous and worried. Jason felt that Selina did not respect him and decided to ignore her. Jason's close friend, Sam, who lived in Brisbane, suggested that he stop talking to Selina, but Jason struggled, as he knew Selina might be telling the truth.

Jason's birthday was in June. When Selina prayed and praised her God, a picture came up in her mind—she virtually saw Jason cuddling a girl, very closely. Since then, Selina suddenly rarely saw

Jason in her dreams. Over the previous years, she had been seeing Jason in more than half her dreams.

In October, Jason uploaded a few photos of himself with a girl. From photos with her best friends who all looked 19-23, you can be certain that she was about 19-23 years' old—so let's call her "the teenager". For an hour, Selina examined all the photos: Jason usually looked sweet, but this 40-year-old looked old and haggard standing next to this teenager. 'Perhaps the teenager was Jason's academic student? Perhaps it was a student event?' After examining for an hour, only when Selina magnified the photos and saw the flowers in his clothes did she realise it was a "wedding".

In all photos, no matter her posture or the situation, the teenager always smiled the same wooden, Shrek-like, very big smile. The only photo showing the teenager with a different facial expression was of a very embarrassed smile when her best friends celebrated her "wedding". She looked like she was thinking, *'Telling my best friends I am going to sleep with an old man twice my age? Shame! Disgrace!'* (photo F)

Only very few of her photos were displayed; but even herself could not find her "happier" photo of celebration with best friends to display. In contrast, whenever Jason came by, she always posted the same very big, wooden smile; unfortunately, it was not a "happy" smile either. Try yourself, facing the mirror: happy or excited people do not smile like that. Her very big, unnatural smiles were like the Joker's in classical Batman—if not fixed with chemicals, it needs quite an effort to smile like that.

Men trust women smiling means they are in love. In fact, prostitutes smile the most in the world. Why? Prostitutes smile for presentation; women in love smile for real.

Men also trust women having sex with them mean the women love them. But ask yourself, do you think prostitutes (women who have sex for money and benefits) are in love?

(The above does not imply the concerned teenager was a prostitute or not. The above is a logic to explain humans' behaviour from a macro point of view.)

Another interesting thing: in a usual wedding, a bride must be excited to take a lot of photos with her best friends in the most important day in her life. But for this teenager, in the eight "wedding day" photos she displayed, four were her best friends taking photos … on their own without her! (Now you understand why Selina could not tell it was a wedding day after examining the photos for an hour.) The "bride" was not quite interested to celebrate her "big day" with her best friends, leaving her best friends celebrating without her. Unless she had actually taken few photos with her best friends, but she loved to display her friends' celebration without herself …

You may argue, it only proved that she was ingenuine and not happy to "marry" Jason. But perhaps she would still want to stay in the "marriage" forever? Some women do stay forever in the "marriages" even they had never ever loved the "husbands". However, those women are at least genuinely happy when they marry those men. In contrast, this teenager put a lot of efforts to pretend to be happy in the "wedding".

Marriage fraud is a type of romance scam, in which one spouse is unwittingly taken advantage of by the foreign spouse who feigns romantic interest, typically in order to obtain a country's residency or for money. (The definition of "marriage fraud" varies in different jurisdiction. The above is what we refer to in this book. Please refer to Appendix 2 for more information.)

Marriage fraud plays the same psychology game as other romance scams do. It is based on lies, acting and hollow promises. Therefore, evidences will only show up after the fraudsters get all they want and ready to leave, costing victims most of their wealth and, more importantly, their passion and significant time—which normally spend few years because it takes few years for the fraudsters to, at least, get a permanent spouse visa (or a green card).

So, how to identify marriage fraud before the final tragedy comes? Well, look at documentaries on any tricky crimes, police detectives identify criminals by first observing their personal behaviours, emotions, facial expression, background and possible intentions. After that, getting solid evidences are only the final steps.

Let's apply this to the case. We had read her facial expression and feelings. What about her behaviours?

Half year before this book was published (2 years after Jason "married" the teenager), Jason's family had taken deposit to sell their 4-bedroom, new house in Strathfield at almost 1 million. Inevitably, some of this fund would flow to Jason's family members. However, the transaction was suddenly terminated. Jason suddenly moved from his own aged 2-bedroom, private apartment in the same area to this new, shared 4-bedroom to please her. Advertisements were immediately put on to look for few tenants to share the house.

The stop of selling of the big house had prevented the money from flowing to Jason's family members—his 2-bedroom was not sold either. Is she only too sick of staying with Jason alone in a private place and prefers a shared house? Or is it her first step to take over the big, new house?

Since then, her relationship with Jason did enhance. True, same as giving cash and gifts to a woman with purposes always enhance a relationship … for a while.

(Once again, it is a logic to analyse human behaviour in a macro point of view.)

Possible intentions: let's look back to what happened when Selina first heard Jason had gone with the teenager:

Selina was struggling, arguing with herself: 'Am I certain that the teenager sleeps with Jason for ingenuine purposes? Can I be wrong? Maybe the teenager truly loves Jason?' Selina went to a barbeque Meetup event to meet new friends. Two young men who spoke Cantonese, the same language as Jason and Selina, were saying: 'The woman left my friend after she was granted a marriage permanent visa.'

'Oh my God, that must have destroyed him for years!'

'Yes. Not only that but afterwards, the woman told him she'd only been with him to get a permanent visa. My friend was very angry and slapped her face. She called the police and had an excuse to separate from him and get his money.'

That is what Jason will face … if not worse.

Another young Cantonese man said, 'My girlfriend has just left me. Now she tells me she only approached me for other purposes … Selina, why are you laughing? It's very hurtful!'

Selina laughed because such woman was worthless and did not deserve any man to feel hurt for. 'Sorry, haha. Don't feel hurt for her—because she had never, ever belonged to you.'

That night, Selina prayed to God, 'My merciful God, please tell me the truth. If the teenager is solely with Jason for his wealth, please make me dream of him tonight, and not tomorrow.'

That night, a dream came upon Selina. In the dream, Selina met Jason, and she found evidence to show Jason that the teenager was deceiving him.

Another night, Selina prayed to God, 'My God, Majesty, please tell me the truth. If the teenager is with Jason to migrate to Australia, please, make me dream of Jason and see his face tonight.' And it happened. That night a dream came upon Selina. There, Selina talked to the teenager, asking 'Why are you willing to stay with such an old man?'

The teenager lowered her voice and said secretly, 'The visa.'

You may not necessarily agree the theory of enquiring God, no matter if you are a Christian or not. But if the theory of enquiry into God holds true, then it always holds true. And this meant the teenager was certainly faking the marriage.

And even if you do not believe the above theory, and even if you argue that some women may love men 20 years older than them—if a 60-year-old woman loves an 80-year-old man, the difference is not obvious; but if a 20-year-old woman "loves" a 40-year-old man, then it is twice her age. You can barely find a woman marrying a man twice her age, except with tycoons and in newspapers.

It is especially unusual because, to my knowledge, the teenager had only dated Jason for a few months before she became "engaged" to him and vowed to give up everything for this newly met twice-as-old man. True, it is not necessary to date for long before getting married to make it true love. However, it is very weird for a 20-year-old, educated girl in a developed country to use only few months to decide she wanted to stay with a man she just met for her remaining 80 years.

When I was 20 years old, I was just graduated from university and my eyes were just opened to the new, big world. 'What is this big world like? What are around? What can happen?' I was family-minded, yet marriage was a distance because my mind was not ready—I didn't even know what options were around. Also, I had only experienced puppy loves. When I was 20, why would I use only few months to decide to settle down with a much older man for my next 80 years, like this teenager claimed she did?

While Selina was thinking of these, a lady from Selina's church approached her. 'Selina, I hope you can help me. I hope very much to stay in Australia. I've studied in Australia for a Master's degree for two years, but my permanent visa application has failed. Now, I've paid a guy to pretend to be de facto with me. The de facto spouse visa application requires two Australians to witness our relationship. Selina, please, I hope you can help me. Don't tell anyone.'

Selina said, 'It's a criminal offence for you, the guy and your friends to fake the witness statements. If you do this, you are going against our country, and our country will be against you. You and your friends will go to jail. Why must you come to Australia? There are other countries that you can migrate to legally.'

But the lady ignored her advice.

The recent market price for a woman asking a guy to fake a de facto relationship or marriage to gain permanent visa status is around AUD 100,000, plus application fees to the Immigration Department of around AUD 7,000. All that, with the risk of being prosecuted.

But by providing "services" to Jason, the teenager will get a migration visa for free, with low or no risk of prosecution! What a deal!

Next, personal background: wasn't it obvious that she was an international student? Locals who grew up in Australia make friends with different races. As for this teenager, from her wedding photos, all her best friends were Chinese, not a single friend of other races. International students stay with people of their own race due to language barrier and because they are more used to people of their own country.

In other words, she did not have permanent residency in Australia and marrying Jason would get her that, as long as she stays with him for about 4 years.

Researching from the Internet, there are only limited resources in regard to confirmed marriage fraud cases. There is a known case that a student visa holder committed this. There is also a confirmed case in which the woman married a twice-as-old man. There is also marriage fraud warning by a government about marrying quickly after meeting someone; but Jason's case is different in the way that, apparently, it does not only hit one such characteristic, but all of them. How can one not be sorry for him?

Selina cried. She cried for herself. She cried for Jason. She cried for one year, two years, she cried until this book was written …

Jason was a righteous man. He was sorry for Selina, but he hoped he was right about the teenager. Selina was sorry for Jason, but he thought he was in love with the teenager. At least, he hoped he was.

Jason deeply wishes to be loved by his wife. But he is now exhausting his efforts, money and passion on a liar who has never loved him and never intended to stay with him for the rest of his life.

Getting a permanent visa through marriage typically takes at least four years. Jason was getting old. Now he thought he was in a marriage and was planning to spend his important last years of youth with an ingenuine person who gave him false hope and fake promises. Jason could lose his last chance to have children because of that.

Finally, getting solid evidence is the last step. Unfortunately, for marriage fraud, solid evidence will only appear at least after fraudsters get Australian permanent residency and victims' wealth— which takes 4 years, and a few years more if she is after more of victim's houses and wealth. (It depends on your country's spouse visa processing time.) Once the damage is done, apparently, there is no legal recourse to reverse the situation. There are not many laws protecting marriage fraud victims, at least not what I know of.

However, I don't mean this girl is a marriage fraudster. Strictly speaking, it is not correct to say so until Jason loses everything, which will not possibly happen until he wastes 2 to 6 more years.

Before this book was written, Selina had been silent for 2 years, again. As time passes, now, Jason seems to have noticed that the teenager has never been genuine; but he has also become even more reluctant to accept the fact that he has wasted years, all his efforts, money and passion on hollow promises and fake love.

Day and night for months or years—it looks realistic

Marriage fraud victims are facing and building relationship with fraudsters day and night for years—look realistic. How can they accept they have been scammed? Same as romance scam victims, who are talking to and building relationship with fraudsters day and night for months or years—look realistic. How can they accept they have been scammed?

In romance scams, including marriage fraud, victims will only invest more and more, with the hope that one day their "lovers" are eventually found to be real, and so as their promises. Unfortunately, fake people will never become real no matter how much efforts victims invest.

Now, what should Selina do??? Wait for Jason, who would not possibly come back that year or next, and might not even survive after that??? Or go with Frederick whom she did not love???

So, let's go back to the topic. Frederick!

Fake company website

Selina was constantly checking whether this Frederick was real or fake.

Back in the first week Selina knew Frederick, she was approached by another man Jonathan on Meetup.com, who also "happened" to claim he was living in Manhattan—this was a warning sign. First, how frequently would foreign men 20 hours' flight away approach ladies in a country of far, far away? Second, Manhattan is not a residential area, yet these two guys happened to live there and both happened to encounter Australian Selina on Meetup.com within two weeks.

Maybe Frederick and Jonathan were both scammers, from the same criminal group, using the same method to attack people on Meetup.com? This way, they could save some effort thinking about their stories. Selina had recently quit and re-joined a group there—possibly Jonathan was confused and thought she was a new member, safe to attack.

Selina was worried. That night, she talked to Frederick, 'Good morning, my love … Sorry, my love, to ensure my safety, can you give me proof that you live in Manhattan New York, and that you are a civil engineer? It is for my safety. I hope you understand.'

'Sure,' Frederick replied.

A few minutes later, Frederick sent her his company website: *http://www.sommiengineeringgroup.com*

Selina examined the website. It was professional-looking, with company details, menus, company expertise, and areas explaining what this company specialised in. There were 14 men's faces in the management team, and Frederick's was one of them. But Selina noticed a few unusual things:

i) She searched for this website using Google and could not find it. The purpose of creating a company website is to let people find you on the Internet—she studied in university that it was easy to do that. Why did the website creator not do this? If it's not searchable, what's the use of this website?

ii) In the contact information, there was a map pinpointing many office locations for this company. So many civil engineering offices of the same group in the New York CBD? Even fast food restaurants might not have that many outlets. Even if it were true, why was the map unclickable? And none of them had a full address listed?

Technically, it is super easy to create a complex, professional-looking fake website. In contrast, legitimate company websites are harder to create. However, it was the first time Selina had encountered an illegitimate website, so she was not fully certain she had sufficient proof to say it was fake. Frederick had not asked for money yet, so Selina did not trace this down further.

Frederick said, 'You shouldn't have asked me for these. Just as I have never asked you for proof.'

But it was he who had approached Selina first. He was more likely to be fake than her.

Selina found Frederick's website suspicious, but she said, 'Thank you for doing this. Have a good day today and work well!'

As time goes by ...

Selina did not want to break the relationship by raising the problem unless she had sufficient evidence against Frederick. But when time went by, Selina got used to Frederick and forgot about all these small and suspicious things.

Potential victims should list out all the problems **at one go**, then it will be obvious that their lovers are fake.

Are you Jason or Frederick?

Not only was Frederick a civil engineer and a Christian as Jason was, but Frederick's company name also happened to be "Sommi Engineering Group" while Jason's was "Somm Engineers". One letter's difference. What a crazy coincidence???

Comparing Jason and Frederick, Frederick was an independent civil engineer in oil rigs, and Frederick was a boss with employees. Selina thought, 'Education background does make a difference. Jason has Master's degrees but he is no independent engineer, while Frederick became an independent engineer at such a young age. Frederick must have studied for an even higher qualification. He studied in Turkey as well.'

In a few photos, Frederick seemed good-looking. But compared with Jason, Selina still felt that Jason's face was much closer to hers. Sometimes, when Selina glanced at a mirror, she thought it was Jason walking by!

Frederick never knew about the existence of Jason, but it happened that he made up stories that matched Jason's background. You may think this was Selina's misfortune. Who knows? The crime turned out to be Selina's salvation at the end of the day.

That nice, well-educated gentleman, Frederick

Frederick always behaved politely and considerately. His writing was elegant, that of a very well-educated man. The music he sent her in earlier days was very American. Even his name: he had another name, Frederico, that seemed very Westernised.

Unusual ... but insignificant

However, Selina occasionally found something unusual: while he occasionally wrote very elegant English, why did his other writing usually have minor English mistakes? Was he too lazy to type? Or he was just too awful in languages, so his English did not look native even though he'd grown up in the United States? Another weird thing was, while he always spoke as a very good, considerate Christian, Selina could sense some of his behaviours were different from a usual, good Christian; yet, these problems were not obvious.

Compared to Jason … Jason was a very genuine, good-hearted and innocent man. Selina always found him sweet—yes, it can be inappropriate to describe a 40-year-old man as "sweet", but he was only two years older than her, so she didn't find him old … okay, only a little bit.

Not sure if Jason is still the good person that she knew … since ruined by a liar.

Selina had never found anything unusual about Jason. But for Frederick, Selina occasionally felt there was something unusual about him, though it wasn't obvious and not sufficient to say he was fake.

The fact is, genuine people are always genuine. But fake people, no matter how hard they act and lie, always have "a number of small things" that are weird.

Body spa

'Sorry Frederick, I need to go now. I want to have a facial and a body spa.'

'Your responsibility ☺.' Frederick replied.

'Good night (and good morning for you in US time).'

'Good night, my queen.'

When Selina came back from Macau to Australia, she bought facial and body spa machines. Usually, women only do facials, but Selina felt that the skin on her legs wasn't nice and bought a new body spa machine to improve it. She only used this body spa machine for those few months—not before this, and not after this.

Doing the body spa, Selina said to herself, 'My responsibility. What does that mean?'

… (Spa machine sound)

'Hang on, why am I doing this body spa? Ladies don't usually use a body spa. Who would? Brides!!'

… (Spa machine sound)

'So, I'm going to be a bride? I'm really going to be a bride? I've started preparing myself to be a bride, and I didn't know that!'

Another coincidence

Selina asked, 'You said you go to church on Sundays. Which type of church do you go to? Baptist, Anglican, Pentecostal or Methodist?'

Selina had spent most of her years in Baptist churches, but had only gone to Anglican churches in recent years. But she'd always considered herself Pentecostal, the church she went to since high school. This was not published anywhere in her Facebook nor Meetup profile—nowhere at all. Even her best friends might not have known she classified herself as Pentecostal.

'I go to Pentecostal church,' Frederick replied.

Selina was surprised: No one knows my background. He really is for me. He's a replacement for Jason!

Marrying, but not for love

Selina struggled. She asked herself: If I am to marry Frederick, am I going to hope Jason and the teenager stay happily ever after?

Answer: NO! This matter is wrong always. Always wrong!

Selina struggled. She asked herself: If I marry Frederick, and then the teenager dumps Jason, am I going to divorce Frederick? If not, who is going to love Jason and take care of him for the rest of his life?

Answer: NO. Unfortunately, this was what Jason had chosen. What did I wish to do when I was 20 years old? Settle down with a 40-year-old guy? Are you crazy? But Jason believes it. Frederick at least makes a good decision and chose me. I cannot let him down.

Selina struggled. She asked herself: If Frederick and I do go on smoothly, can I not be angry with God anymore about Jason? Can I recover, go back to church and worship God as I had for the past 30 years?

Answer: NO. Wrong is wrong. Jason should not be with the teenager and I should not be with Frederick. The whole matter is just wrong, wrong, WRONG. Maybe I will gradually, gradually recover, but I can't see this happening.

Selina decided to go with Frederick. Perhaps, she just wanted to end her pain by convincing herself that Jason had never been the one. Or, perhaps, she just wanted to prove the opposite—Frederick or other men would never work out with her, no matter how hard she tried.

Since Jason had chosen to stay with the teenager, Selina had not prayed much and rarely enquired her God, at least, not in this instance. If she did, she would have known Frederick was a fake.

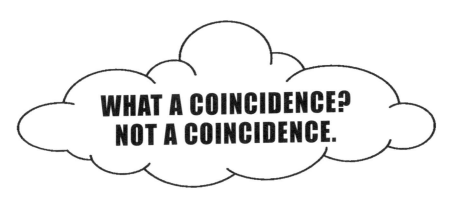

WHAT A COINCIDENCE? NOT A COINCIDENCE.

In a romance scam, it is **very usual** that you find the man/ woman you met online has a very similar background as yourself. If you have included your hobbies, background, photos or personal opinions on Facebook, any dating profiles or any other profiles on the Internet, scammers will tailor their backgrounds to match yours.

For example, if your profile says you are a Christian, love playing piano and have a Chinese background, then he/she would claim that they are a Christian, love listening to music and love Chinese food—making you feel that he/she is a rare match for you.

You will feel that he/she is tailor-made for you, because indeed, he/ she was manually tailor-made for you in this virtual environment.

This same trick is also used in certain magic or real-life divination performances.

Unfortunately, in Selina's case, she hadn't disclosed what she thought on any Internet platform, nor even to friends, and Frederick just guessed randomly. And unfortunately, Frederick's criminal group did happen to take a similar company name as Jason's company—when they never even knew there was a Jason!

Sometimes unfortunate coincidences do happen in scams.

WE ARE GETTING
MARRIED IN AUGUST

Wedding plans

Maybe, Jason will never come back, so God has given me a replacement for him, Frederick.

Marrying you does not necessarily mean I love you. You can be only a replacement. Or, like what the teenager does …

'So, where do you want to settle down after we get married?' Frederick asked.

'Where do you prefer? Australia or the United States?'

'I'll let you decide, my heart. I am an independent civil engineer. No problem for me to get work wherever I go.'

It sounded like Frederick really respected Selina much. According to him, he had no close living family at all (he said he only had cousins around the United States in different areas whom he only met once a year). So it was not surprising he was so kind to Selina and treated her as his only family. Poor man, he must be very lonely to be willing to give up his New York home for her.

Selina said, 'I prefer Australia. The environment is better—less pollution, nice people, laidback culture.'

'Great, then we'll settle in Australia after we get married.'

'Okay. My plan is that we date in New Zealand and Australia. If we feel good about each other, then after your three-four months' work in New Zealand, we can have our wedding in New York. Your friends and cousins can celebrate with you. Of course, I'll arrange for my parents to be there as well. The next year, we can have another banquet in Macau with my friends and relatives.'

'I hope we can wed in Australia. Because the visa application takes time. If we wed late, we will need to be separated once we get married.'

*** Frederick asked to wed as soon as possible to immerse his victims deep into beautiful dreams. This way, when he asks to "borrow" money from them or carry bags through customs for him, victims can hardly refuse. Otherwise, it is like you are, by your own hand, breaking your own dreams. ***

Research: his story sounds valid

Selina did more research on his field—oil rigs. Yes, there are oil rigs in both the United States and New Zealand.

Now, is this industry bigger in the United States or Australia? Indeed, the United States has much higher oil production. Australia has a lot of natural resources but not much oil. She also checked whether he required any additional license or qualifications to open a civil engineering practice in Australia.

'Honey, you are very American,' said Selina.

'We are both American. You are going to marry an American engineer, so you are also American.'

'I remember last year when I visited Ellis Island National Museum of Immigration in New York. Men looked at photos to choose women as their wives. By the time those ladies arrived at New York port and they met for the first time in person, they were about to get married.'

'Yes, I follow the US tradition.'

Guaranteed permanent residency in the United States

Selina said, 'Honey, I've thought more about it. You have your cousins in the United States, and your workers, and your office, and your friends. As for me, I don't actually have that much support in Australia. I'm willing to move to New York for you.'

Selina really didn't want to move to the United States. Moving to New York is a fantastic dream for many Chinese girls, but to Selina, it would be a sacrifice—she personally loved Australia much more.

'Great! I love the United States. Let's settle in New York, my home, then!' Frederick said.

She checked out the United States' government websites. There were a few visa options but yes, it would normally take a while—around 9 months or more.

So, it was really better to get married as soon as possible, so that they would not need to be separated for too long. It would be best to marry in August. They would have two months to get to know each other in person before getting to the wedding, then Frederick could immediately apply for a US marriage visa for Selina. When he left New Zealand at the end of October, they would only need to be separated for seven months. Alternatively, Selina could possibly get a temporary visa to the US for about six months. Then, they'd barely need to be separated.

'My love, I know you're busy with work. I've checked out the procedure to get a marriage visa for me to the United States and found out how long it will take. I think you need to sign the paperwork now, before you leave the United States.'

'That's alright, honey, leave the US visa thing to me. I'll sort it out. You concentrate on our wedding plans. Okay?'

'Okay.'

'Honey, your US residence is secured!'

Wedding plans

< Selina thought: I like vineyards. Maybe we can have our wedding in a vineyard? I'll arrange for my parents to come to Australia for our wedding. My elderly father rarely takes a flight, so I'll get him business class. He's old—I can't let him suffer the long flight in economy. As for my mother, who frequently travels, I'll only get her economy … But my father is such a gentleman. He'll probably give his spot in business class to my mother and go in economy himself!

I'll tell them that father must take business class, or I'll be angry!

Friends … I will only invite my friends in Australia. They're in Brisbane, Melbourne and Perth. We'll stay in vineyard accommodation for two-three nights as hospitality.

Or maybe we should wed at a church? I am still angry with God, but He should still have a place in my life on such an important occasion.>

Selina asked Frederick, 'Love, would you prefer to get married in a church? Or another place, like a vineyard or by the sea?'

'You decide, my queen.'

'Then let's get married in a church.'

Selina emailed her previous church, Pastor Richard, about an arrangement to wed in August.

'The first two weeks do not work for me. What about the third weekend? I can do either Saturday or Sunday,' Pastor Richard said.

'Ok. Saturday then—18 August.'

'Yes. In terms of arrangements, both of you will need to bring your identification and proof of address. Also, I have attached a form required by government … And before the wedding, we need to have a wedding consultation with both of you.'

'Must we have the consultation? My fiancé will be working in New Zealand and can't come over to meet with you easily.' And Selina was also tired of the church's commands since Jason left.

'Okay. We could also do it through a video conference, or over email. And there's a fee for weddings at our church, of AUD 600.'

'Sure. That sounds good.'

< Selina thought: So, the wedding plans were done. Next: more on the arrangement for my parents. They will come on Wednesday or Thursday, or even earlier if they like. My home is small, so they'll stay in the lounge nearby. My best friends in Australia, Evita and Anna, would also come from other states. On the wedding day, we'll hire a car and a driver to get to the church—I don't want the groom nor the bride to drive on the wedding day. Nor my old father. I don't trust Evita's driving, as she rarely drives in built-up areas, and Anna too rarely drives.

After the wedding, we will stay in the beautiful Hunter Valley for two days as a celebration and to let my parents get to know Frederick more. It will also be our short honeymoon.

In the Hunter Valley, there is alpaca farm accommodation. The Chinese find this animal amazing because it looks like a sheep, but is not a sheep; and looks like a horse, but is not a horse. It is actually a camelid. There are no alpacas in China, so they are considered a "magical" animal that exists but appears virtual to them. Most Chinese never see a real one in their lives. The alpaca farm stay would be fantastic. And there are many vineyards around too. I love vineyards!!! I love vineyards!!! Beautiful layouts, excellent food, elegant landscapes.

I don't really care about having a long honeymoon in a far-away country, as we have been travelling too much already. I just want to settle down. I'm tired. >

Wedding dress

The entire wedding rundown was settled. Now that Selina had spare time, she started browsing for a wedding dress.

A while ago, Selina's previous best friend Gen said, 'If I am to get married, I will ask my husband to choose a wedding dress for me.'

Selina said to Gen, 'If I am to marry Jason, I will choose an elegant, long, long wedding dress.'

< Selina thought: Now I am going to marry Frederick. This short, elegant one will be fine. >

No need to work after marrying

'My love, tell me more about your work. Do you always go to oil rigs for a few months?'

'Well,' Frederick said tenderly, 'I am a civil engineer. My main work is on oil rigs and pipeline installation. But I also build roads and bridges.'

'Really? I previously worked in a construction company, and we built bridges as well.'

'Wah! So, about the travelling, I sometimes send my workers to the oil rigs. For myself, I usually do about one long trip for a few months once or twice a year.'

'That's great! I thought you'd go away all around the year and I'd be like a widow most of the time.'

'Don't worry. You know what? Actually, I don't want you to work after we wed. I hope you just stay at home. Or you can be my secretary so that I can see you every day.'

'Not working would be boring. And I don't want to be your secretary—owning a business is stressful and tedious. I'd like to do the usual computer work that I do.'

'Okay, okay. I respect you. '

''

'You're going to be a happily married woman, with children to take care of.'

'★'

Children

'Honey,' said Frederick, 'my parents said that my wife will have twins.'

'Really? That's incredible!!'

'Yes. Actually, I had a twin sister. She died soon after she was born.'

Selina was frustrated. Frederick was such an unlucky guy. So many people around him died! She hoped he wouldn't bring her bad luck.

Selina acted as if everything was alright. 'Honey, can I look at your photos with your parents?' Selina was family-minded and admired her fiancé's parents.

'I left them in Los Angeles. I'll get them for you when I go to Los Angeles. I will. I will.'

< Selina thought: Strange. You said you loved your parents so much and you even cried on Mother's Day because you missed them. How can you not have any of their photos with you and have left them in a place four hours' flight away? >

Frederick could not read Selina's mind. Frederick felt that Selina now fully trusted him as she had started planning their wedding and was looking forward to a perfect marriage with kids. It was the perfect time for him to do what he'd always intended to do ...

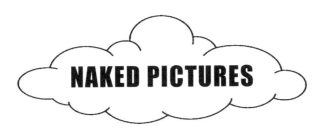

NAKED PICTURES

No matter if it is a romance scam or your real lover, even if you sincerely believe that you are going to marry him/her, never send a single naked picture with your face.

It is very dangerous to send naked pictures or similar material through the Internet. It can lead to blackmail, and no matter how much money you pay, you can never buy them back, as infinite copies can be made and sent anywhere in the world, including to your friends, colleagues or family.

Even in real life, it is best not to take such photos or record such videos … unless you are expecting them to be made public ^.^!

(If you have already sent out naked pictures to scammers, this is likely to end in disaster. Maybe try to play dumb? Or scam your scammer, pretending you don't know they are scammers, and hope they forget that one day? But there is no known precedent that this will work …)

EVIDENCE

So much evidence? Or so many fake documents?

Ecclesiastes 9: 11 'I returned, and saw under the sun, that the race is not to the swift, nor the battle to the strong, neither yet bread to the wise, nor yet riches to men of understanding, nor yet favour to men of skill: but time and chance happeneth to them all.' - King Solomon

Scammers do not need to be cleverer nor more skilful than you; they just know the tricks, and you don't.

A red flag or he's just unlucky?

'Good morning, my love. How r u today?' Selina asked Frederick.

'I'm fine, dear … Honey, there is something urgent I'd like you to do for me.'

< *Selina thought: It must be either i) he is not coming to New Zealand any more or ii) he wants to borrow money—meaning he is probably a scammer. Either i) or ii), would be terrible.* >

'Honey, I ordered my materials from Singapore. There's still some owing, but it's going to take too long to transfer the money from New York. I've run out of time—can you make the payment from Australia for me?'

Frederick continued, 'Honey, it's not much, I've made most the payment already, but it's urgent. I can't do the transfer myself cos it'll take too much time from the US to APAC.'

< *Selina thought: Ha, why is this even my problem?* >

She said, 'Honey, my bank account is also not in Singapore. The timeframe for me to pay Singapore from Australia is the same as your timeframe to pay from New York.'

'Really?'

'I think so. It's a foreign bank transfer anyway.'

'Honey, don't worry. I think yours would be faster.'

'Definitely it can't possibly be faster from me. But I think there are different bank transfer methods. I think it should only take one to three days from the US.'

'Last week, I made a transfer from New York to China. It took 7 days to arrive. My love, please help me. It's not a huge amount this time, only SGD 7,500.'

'That's crazy. It's got no relation to geographical distance. Must be your bank or your transfer method. Use a credit card or BPAY or something like that. That'll be the fastest.'

'You mean Bitcoin?'

Selina didn't even know what Bitcoin was. She searched for information on how to do a quick money transfer so that Frederick could resolve the problem himself. Then she sent him a URL. 'Try this. There are money transfer agents who can do it very quickly in New York.'

'Honey, I don't want to have any app on my phone that's not advised by my bank. It's for security reasons. I hope you understand.'

'If there is no other way, would you consider physically going to Singapore to do the transfer yourself? But why has the amount suddenly increased? Is everything safe?'

'It's because of inflation ... Honey, like I said before, don't worry. Let's just give it a try from your side and see what happens.'

Address search: highly suspicious, but no solid evidence

< *Selina thought: It's really his own concern. Why is it even related to me??? >*

Frederick continued, 'You know how much I love you? If it was you who needed this transfer, I'd do it for you.'

'Give me your full home address.'

'I live at 77 Water Street, Manhattan, New York.'

Selina searched the web and thought of her trip to New York last year. Once again, she wanted to prove Frederick was lying, but couldn't think of how to. So, she directly said, 'You don't live at 77 Water Street. My hotel was the next street from there during my last New York trip. 77 Water Street is a commercial building. You lied to me.'

'Sorry, it's my office address.'

< *Selina thought: I knew you'd say that. But I just can't prove you lied … >*

(Selina should have been tougher and not even let him explain. If she'd been informed that romance scams were common, she would have already dropped off.)

She said, 'It's still wrong. Last time, you sent me a photo where you were outside your office *(photo C)*. 77 Water Street doesn't look like that.'

'I was out for a conference meeting in that photo.'

< *Selina thought: I knew you'd say that. How can I prove you lied? >*

Selina searched the web, hoping to see details on what companies there were at 77 Water Street, but she couldn't find anything. There was only a GPS photo of 77 Water Street.

'My home address is Adams str APT Brooklyn NT 11201 … Honey, so much stress from you. Have you done the transaction yet?'

'You said you live in a house. This address is an apartment.'

'No, it's a house.'

Now it was a problem between two stupid people—Frederick, an uneducated, uncivilized rat in a third-world country, didn't know that APT refers to "apartment". Selina, who knew APT referred to apartment, thought that APT might or might not have another meaning in New York. Maybe it was an abbreviation for something else?

As in a court, without sufficient proof, Selina thought she could only assume Frederick was innocent. (Sorry, I shouldn't give myself an excuse here!) Selina never loved Frederick, but at that stage, she did hope Frederick was real—she was expecting a marriage, a family called "home" for her to settle down in. For years and years, she'd been tired.

LinkedIn search: slightly suspicious

Frederick said that the recipient was his work agent. Her name was Ling Tien Tien. Selina searched if there's such a person's information on the Internet. Indeed, there was a "Ling Tien Tien" in LinkedIn who worked in the oil and pipeline area in Singapore … but Selina wasn't sure it was legitimate. Something looked suspicious. (I won't disclose details here as scammers may also be reading this book.)

Frederick had given the bank account address: "Blk 548 Cha Chu Kang". Indeed, Selina had been working in Singapore for a few weeks and just came back to Sydney last week. She'd never been to Cha Chu Kang in Singapore, but according to Google maps, that was a bit remote. Google search did not have a photo of that place. So, no hints.

Now that Selina wasn't in Singapore, she had no other means to find out whether this address was valid or not and what "Blk 548 Cha Chu Kang" was. But that was only a bank to bank transfer which is relatively secure, not sending money via Western Union. Also, Singapore is a developed country. The recipient bank Singapore ICBC was regulated and was supposed to have done customer due diligence to ensure the bank account owner was legitimate.

One-off gambling

Selina checked the Internet: what Frederick claimed may be valid. It really was possible for some banks to take a few days to do an international transfer, as they hold the money to offer short-term loans to other customers to gain a high interest rate—so evil! Selina'd previously worked in banks and knew it could be practical.

Most people will tell you, if you are lending money to someone, give yourself a number and decide you must not exceed it. That was also what Selina thought. But she didn't understand paying a little would lead directly to paying her life savings.

< *Selina thought: Frederick says SGD 7,500 is a small number; it's not small to me. But okay. I'll only give him SGD 7,500. That's it!*

After all, he is asking me to send money to Singapore, and it happens that I frequently travel there for business. As I've worked for a few Singapore enterprises over the years, I almost feel I am like a Singaporean permanent resident or citizen, although I have never been one. Why did Frederick happen to ask me to send money to Singapore, not another country? I wouldn't be doing it if it were a country that I wasn't familiar with, but with Singapore, I am. >

Selina made the SGD 7,500 transfer.

After that, Frederick and Selina went back to honeymoon time. Frederick loved Selina and cared about everything she did. He greeted her every morning and evening, telling her his future dreams with her. 'Selina, don't talk when you are eating. We'll talk after you finish your breakfast.' Looks like he was a really well-educated, well-mannered man.

Three days later, Frederick said, 'Honey, can you help me to transfer SGD 1,500 more?'

Selina was unwilling, but compared with SGD 7,500, SGD 1,500 wasn't much.

Selina went to her bank and made this SGD 1,500 transfer.

Frederick smiled sarcastically, 'Hahahaha, it's SGD 15,000, not SGD 1,500.'

'SGD 15,000???? That may be a small number to you, but it's a huge number to me!'

Selina disliked his sarcastic smile, but she thought, *'What if what he said was true?'* After all, she had promised (SGD 1,500) and she didn't want to "change her mind" and deny him. She didn't like disappointing friends.

US passport & US banking documents

Now Selina was about to put herself into a trap …

'If you want me to make this transfer, you must give me proof of your address. Electricity bill, water bill, driver's license, photo ID, whatever. Also, you must transfer the same amount to me now – including the last SGD 7,500. You must transfer a total of SGD 22,500 now, before I do the SGD 15,000 for you.'

'Honey, all my proof of address documents are at my office. It's midnight.'

'Midnight is not a problem. If you consider this urgent, then do things urgently yourself, don't push me to do everything for you urgently. You live very close to your office. Go to your office now to get the identity and address documents and do the transfer to me. It's midnight, so take your dog with you for safety.'

< *Selina thought: What he said could happen … but no, it couldn't.* >

The next morning, she asked, 'You drive to work. How come you don't even have your driver's license with you???'

'You only want my driver's license? Here it is.'

Frederick sent her a copy of his US passport (*photo E*), and a banking document from JP Morgan Chase *(photo G)* that he had already sent her USD 113,000.

Selina was glad. <*She thought: He loves me so much! He asked me to transfer SGD 22,000 for him, but he gave me USD 113,000. The remaining part must be for the wedding costs and the bride fee.*>

In Chinese culture, a groom normally needs to pay a handsome bride fee to the bride's father to show that he is grateful the father has brought up the lovely bride and has taken care of her.

So, Selina immediately transferred the funds for him. <*She thought: When I look for a job, my foreign agents ask me for my passport copy, then I get the job. No one has ever questioned if the copy of my passport is fake. Now Frederick has given me a copy of his passport. I'm not going to expect it is fake: If I expect it's fake, then why did I even ask for it? Further, if he fakes it, he'll fake it professionally and I as a layman won't be able to tell.* >

The only checking she did was to examine the graphic patterns on his passport and his passport photo (*photo E*). <*Selina thought: Look at his facial expression and the way he looked at camera. If it's a fake passport, then the passport photo probably doesn't belong to the person talking to me and was only downloaded from the web. People normally smile or have other facial expressions when taking a usual photo, but in this passport photo, he really didn't smile and looked directly at the camera. It really is likely to be a real passport photo.>* And when she magnified it, it did have some patterns on it, like a usual passport.

It happened that Selina's phone was down—the telco had a big technical problem. All customers with a recent change plan could only use data but couldn't make any calls at all. Otherwise, Selina would have called US migration to verify if the passport was real or fake.

You may be wondering why so many unfortunate coincidences in this true story happened to Selina. And I can tell you, I was wondering the same!

A few days later, Frederick asked for another SGD 51,000 transfer. Selina immediately did it without a thought, as the total was still below the USD 113,000 that his US banking document indicated he'd already sent her. However, an error message came up in the Internet banking, saying Selina's daily limit was AUD 50,000 (SGD was slightly higher than AUD at banking rate at that time). So, Frederick asked her to do SGD 49,000 for the day and the rest in another transaction the next day.

Frederick's new workplace in New Zealand

Things seemed to have got back to normal. Frederick told Selina his plans on how to meet in New Zealand next weekend. He reminded her to check the local weather before booking her own flight.

'We don't need to meet in Auckland every week. From New Plymouth airport, you can also fly to Wellington. That way we could visit a different place, as we're both taking flights anyway,' Selina suggested.

'Sure, and some weeks you can just come to Awakino. I'll show you the area I work in. And I'll come to Australia to stay with you on other weekends.'

(He said this rubbish to make Selina believe that he was there for her, not for her money.)

The cycle of gambling addiction

A few days later, Frederick asked her to transfer an additional SGD 30,700. That made the accumulated amount almost equivalent to USD 113,000—the amount that Frederick claimed to have already sent her.

Selina didn't want to do this transfer—it should never have been her problem. But because he'd shown her his banking document claiming that he'd already sent her USD 113,000, which was in transit, it had now become her problem.

< *Now Selina was worried: I thought he sent me USD 113,000 for the wedding or the bride fee to my father. But he actually sent me the banking document because he wants me to send out the same amount????? It might be fraud!!! That means I have already lost SGD 74,500???*

But what if it is not fraud, and he was just in a terrible rush and didn't consult me before his actions? If he did send me USD 113,000, making his own pocket empty, and now I don't send out my money for him, then his business is going to crash, because he trusted me????? I have already paid SGD 74,500. Now, there is only SGD 30,700 to go … >

Selina definitely didn't want to make this transfer.

Frederick talked tenderly to her, showing he cared about her as if nothing had happened. On the other hand, he occasionally changed topics to continue to persuade her. 'I'm not well.'

'What's happening?'

'Honey, you're funny. My project is going to die. How can I be happy?'

Selina didn't like the way he spoke to her sarcastically. Frederick had previously used the word "funny" to praise Selina's lovely nature.

'I have spent so much effort in the past months to get this contract and did a great deal of preparation. Now, because of a little bit of money, my project is going to die. You can guess how I must feel.'

'Your money is supposed to get to me on Friday, after that, I can do the transfer for you.'

'That'll be too late. My project deadline is Friday, New Zealand time. You will miss the deadline. Honey, it's OUR project. Please help, please.'

'You're only an engineer. Why do you need to pay your money before doing the job?'

'It's part of the deal. They want to test my ability to manage money and things. In this job, I need to first pay for the materials, and then there'll be a settlement and they will pay me a huge amount of money soon. If I fail to do this, then they'll consider me as having broken the contract, and all the effort I've spent for the past few months will go down the drain.'

Selina checked on the Internet to see if what he said could be possible, but there was no clear information about whether or not this type of contract exists.

'When is the settlement day?'

'Friday (tomorrow).'

'You are sure that's the last payment for your materials?'

'100% sure.'

Pretty close: real-time video call

Selina was still worried. She pressed the button for video call in Whatsapp with Frederick. But Frederick didn't answer.

He said, 'Honey, what are you doing? I've told you I don't like doing video calls.' Indeed, he had never said so as they'd never discussed this topic before.

Selina replied, 'I want to ensure you are you. Please.'

Selina continued to press the video conference button a few times, and Frederick continued to reject her calls.

'I hate video calls. I've never done it in my life!' said Frederick, 'My mother warned me about video calls. I don't know. I've never done it. I'm afraid!'

'You said I am your wife-to-be. Why do you fear making a real-life video call with your wife-to-be? Please, please, I really want to help you. Once you do a conference call with me, then I can be certain you are real and will send the money out.' Selina begged him to do a real-life video call: she really wanted to prove he was real—she didn't want to know that he was a fake and she'd already lost SGD 74,500!

'I've told you, I'm afraid of video calls. It's just money, and I don't like to be insulted! Now, I'm going to work, feeling really disappointed.'

< Selina thought: He wouldn't do a real-time video call. Okay, then I couldn't confirm he was real. So I wouldn't make the transfer. >

A few minutes later, Frederick sent out a personal video *(video 2)*— he was driving an open-deck car, smiling at the camera, driving to his office, as he'd said he would. Selina looked at the background. *< She thought: California? Yellow, sandy and dusty. It feels like the Hollywood or Los Angeles area? Or, maybe he happens to be driving through an area in New York that has this type of view? >* Looking at the map of New

York, driving from Brooklyn to 77 Water Road was not likely to go through this kind of landscape, but … she wasn't certain.

'This is what I can do for us. No matter what happens, your USD 113,000 will arrive on Friday US time—Monday your time. But I love you. You take care.' Which implied that if Selina insisted on not making the transfer, his project would fail and he wouldn't meet her in New Zealand any more.

< *Selina re-examined the video and thought: who could have this kind of personal video? If he was not the person in the video, then he must be a person very close to the person in the video. Even if it was a trap, it was still very close hints.*

She thought: He provided a US passport and banking documents from JP Morgan Chase. If it is really a fraud, I am still protected under law.

She thought: Some people do have phobias about something unreasonably. Like, I hate geckos. Is it because a gecko can kill me? No. No reason. I just hate them. And Frederick has a phobia about video calls. But this personal video is almost equivalent to a personal video. Maybe I should accept it … >

** Refer to the last page of the book - Clarifications

Privacy

Due to privacy reasons, I fell victim

The following morning, she took a few hours off to go to the Australian branch of his bank, JP Morgan Chase, to verify whether his banking document was real or fake.

'We're JP Morgan. We don't have Chase, the traditional bank, in Australia. Here's the 24-hour US phone number that you can call, but they may not tell you anything as they may not be able to disclose their customer information.'

'Thank you,' said Selina.

Government websites didn't help

Then she tried another option—according to the Internet, any foreign transfer would first be settled at the Reserve Bank. So, Selina went to Australian Reserve Bank to check this out.

An officer of the Reserve Bank said, 'No, the money does not actually settle here. Let me look at your banking document ... I can't tell whether it's real or not. Where did you get it from again?'

Selina explained to them what happened. They said, 'You haven't met him in person? Then it's likely to be a scam. Probably he is from Nigeria?' ("Probably" means maybe or maybe not.)

'Nigeria??? Can't be? I've been talking to him for months. And what is the meaning of scam?'

'Fraud. Here is a government website, Scamwatch. Have a look.'

Selina looked at the website—long essays! She studied it but didn't "happen" to come across what Frederick had done, so she thought it was okay. If Selina had a few days to study those long essays, maybe she would have found something. Obviously, criminals would not give victims so much time to decide.

Photo check—no information

She also did a Google search on the three photos of Frederick, as per the few scam alert websites suggested. But nothing hit.

Insufficient evidence against Frederick— What if he is telling the truth???

There was not much time left. If Frederick's story was real, she had to make a decision to do the transfer in one hour. The last thing she could check was to call Chase in the United States. But her phone was still down and unable to make any calls at all.

Selina went to a telco branch and showed them her staff card. 'I'm your customer, and your consultant. I have an urgent call to make to the United States. I've paid fees but your network has failed. Can I borrow a phone?'

A customer service guy said, 'No. Our landline cannot make international calls.'

'Then can I borrow your personal phone for one single urgent call? I'm your customer and have paid my fees. Your telco has failed to provide the service I've paid for. And I'm your consultant.'

'No. It's my own mobile phone. You can't use it. Let me figure it out for you.'

'Your technical team had attempted to fix my phone a few times, but they all failed. You're customer service. You won't be able to fix it. Please try other options. You won't be able to fix my phone. Or do I need to get a new prepaid number?'

'Sure, just leave it with me.'

Then the customer service guy called their local support a few times. On and off, no luck. He said, 'I'm very kind. I'm doing much to help you.' After half an hour, Selina went to another telco opposite it, who said, 'If you want to transfer your number to our telco, it will take 24 hours. You will only be able to make phone calls after that.' So, it didn't work for Selina.

She went back to her telco. 45 minutes had gone. The customer service guy was still talking to their local support. He said to Selina, 'Can you talk to them please?'

Once she got the call, she knew what he'd been doing. She stood up angrily and yelled at him, 'I've told you, your technical team failed to fix the network many times, and you, customer service, attempted to fix it and made me sit for one hour???? Because you want to save me $40, I'm going to lose $30,700 for you!!!!'

The manager heard her yelling and came over, 'Lady, if you yell at our staff, I will call the police.'

'Yes, please, I really want to talk to the police!' She really hoped to talk to police as she was helpless. Selina showed the manager her staff card, and said, 'I'm your contractor. I'm here to make one single urgent international call. Your staff sat me here for one hour!'

The customer service guy was ashamed. He watched them from a distance, realising that he'd done something very wrong. He was worried, eventually. (He was indeed stupid. It was office hours and he'd wasted an hour of his client's time in an attempt to save $40. Most people earn more than $40 per hour!!)

The manager saw Selina's staff card. He calmed down (and of course, now, he didn't want to call the police any more). 'Then I don't understand. Why don't you use your own phone?'

'That's why I'm here!'

The manager lent his mobile phone to Selina. Selina called US Chase. As expected, Chase said they said they were unable to disclose whether the banking document was real or fake, and could not even disclose whether the customer existed or not due to protection of customer privacy.

Selina could only borrow the phone for one single call; there was no other chance to negotiate with US Chase nor to talk to other people. The customer service guy had wasted an hour when she only had an hour left to decide. She did think of going to the police, but she believed the police would not give her an outcome in only a few minutes. They'd probably take days—which would be no use.

* Refer to the last page of the book - Clarifications

Protected by law in theory, but not in practice

Selina felt helpless. She thought, 'I have spent so much effort to prove Frederick is fake, and I've failed. Now I should assume he's real. What if he did make the USD 113,000 transfer to me and I hold my funds now? Then he is going to fail and lose everything because he knows me? No, I can't let it happen. I have to transfer my money now.'

Selina didn't know Internet romance
scams were so common; if she knew that,
she wouldn't have risked it.

Selina thought, 'If his passport and banking documents are indeed fake, then I am still protected by law and will trace him till the end of the world.'

Selina didn't know she was
only theoretically protected by the law,
and not in practice protected by the law.

Selina thought, 'As long as things can be transmitted through the Internet (he was talking to me in Whatsapp), there must be a trace. It won't be hard to trace him if he is fake.'

Selina was correct that, technically,
there was a trace; but individuals cannot
easily trace this down legally.

Making the decision to make the transfer, different voices were shouting in Selina's brain:

 The voice of her best friend from university, Liam, screamed, 'Selina, it is okay you're looking for love, but be careful of romance fraud. I know you are clever and cautious, but among all the fraud cases that I have seen, he'll only ask you for money when he knows you fully trust him.'

Another voice from Liam, when Selina was leaving Macau to move to Australia, 'Selina, being a new immigrant is not easy. If you encounter financial problems when you're in Australia, tell me, I'm always here to help.'

This is how friends treat each other.

Her other best friend Evita, who was getting married soon, said, 'Selina, it's okay for you to look for a husband, but don't lose money over it. It's okay to lose your body, but promise me, never lose your money!'

A TV drama about enterprise war, which said, 'Losing a great deal of money is not the end of the world. As long as you are hardworking and aggressive, you'll gain it back.'

 A Chinese proverb that says, 'Merit is to choose to be betrayed rather than to betray.'

But there is another Chinese proverb from the famous ancient military genius Cao Cao, 'Better to betray the whole world than to let them betray me!'

Selina recalled, 'Last year, when Jason went with the girl, I attempted suicide. When I wrote my will to say how to distribute my money after I die, I realised that having one or two more digits of money made no difference when I was going to die. If this Frederick is real, I have a chance to live happily ever after; if Frederick is fake, then keeping my money won't bring me much … Go ahead.'

Later, Selina re-watched a few times the video that Frederick had sent her. Selina examined his smile, his facial expression, and sensed, 'Yes, he was smiling at his girlfriend … But … that wasn't me! Some guys love me, but they don't smile at me like this!'

WHY DO VICTIMS PAY THEIR LIFE SAVINGS TO SOMEONE THEY'VE ONLY MET ONLINE?

Scammers always start by asking for a little bit of money, and almost always promise to pay you back. Victims pay the money, not only because of so-called "love", but also because of fake evidence (fake company websites, fake passports, fake banking documents, fake LinkedIn profiles, fake third-party witnesses who actually belong to the same criminal groups). Further, if they don't pay the small amount, they risk losing a happy future with a sincere lover who'll truly love him/her forever.

Once the victim agrees to pay, they'll naturally and subconsciously develop a psychology similar to gambling. Every time victims pay, they subconsciously come to trust him/her even more—coz they do not want to accept the fact that they've already paid money for nothing. If the victims now reject the scammers' further requests, then the amounts they've already paid are definitely lost. If the victim continues to pay, they have "hope" that the online lovers and their stories are actually real and what they've already paid will be rewarded. This gambling psychology is the core reason why so many people end up losing a fortune.

Further, when the amount a victim pays reaches a certain level, say 50% of their life savings, they may naturally stop doubting or questioning the Internet lover. This is because it is too terrifying for them to consider they have already made a huge mistake. So, they'll continue to pay without questioning, or even get conned into drug trafficking or money laundering for their scammers, until they get caught by the police or until they lose their life savings. Some become bankrupt.

Therefore, it is best to not even pay one single cent.

If you have friends or family who you believe have fallen victim to a romance scam, please i) inform them about romance scams and show them relevant websites or news < *you can find more resources at our company website, or you can search for more on the Internet* >; ii) try your very best to find evidence to show them they are scams; iii) seek help from organisations or companies who can capture this evidence, such as our company *Alpaca Consulting IT Pty Ltd*; or iv) seek help from the cybercrime squad in your country (e.g., ACSC) or the police.

DAILY LIFE

Simple things are too difficult for scammers

'What we had encountered looked like a scam; but I knew it wasn't a scam—scams only happen to other people, not us. Frederick, I know you are real. I can tell how sincere you are from your attitude and from your responses. I know you are real. I know how much you care and are concerned about me. I know you truly love me,' Selina thought.

Selina's under a spell

Now Selina was under Frederick's spell.

Before she made the last big transfer, she only half-trusted Frederick. But after she sent out the last amount, SGD 30,700, she subconsciously became fully trusting of him.

Selina had dropped her defences. She could no longer question Frederick. (How could she question herself when she'd already sent out 70% of her own funds if this Frederick was still dubious???)

*** Selina didn't lose her mind for love,
but for her own money on Frederick's hand. ***

Frederick knew he could not use the same excuse to ask for money again. He had told Selina that last Friday was the confirmation day for his work and that had to be the final funds needed to settle his materials in the Asia Pacific region. He decided to move the story forward …

'Honey, I'm very happy about this project.' Frederick implied that her transferring the money had indeed saved his project and brought their future dreams to life.

Selina had talked to her own bank about Frederick's funds, as the expected arrival date had already passed. But the bank couldn't see any such funds arriving at all. The bank told Selina to check with the party who'd sent it to her.

Frederick replied, 'I went to my own bank in person today. They said the funds are still in transit. I am seriously chasing them. I'll take care of it. You don't worry, okay? As I've said before, don't worry about your money. I'm coming to New Zealand with cash. We have many alternatives. Your money is safe.'

Flight

Frederick continued, 'Honey, I've booked my air ticket. I'm flying from New York to New Zealand on Tuesday.'

'It's a direct flight—20 hours.'

'Wah! That's long! Which airline are you taking?'

'Emirates. Business class.'

'Of course, if it's economy class for a 20-hour non-stop direct flight, you'd be really suffering.'

'I have to bear it, dear. The most important thing is to arrive safely so I can see my wife.'

'♡ Can you show me your air ticket so that I know when you'll arrive?'

Frederick sent her an image of his flight booking, but Selina found a few things that looked very wrong. First, this flight from New York to New Zealand would take 20 hours. Not many aircraft can make direct flights of 20 hours without stopping—they can't hold that much fuel. A few months ago, Selina heard there was a new type of aircraft that could do a similar distance without stopping, but it only went from Australia to London, no other known routes.

When she went to the Emirates website to look at something, indeed, there were no direct flights from New York to New Zealand to be found. They had to stop at least once.

Second, SQ25 on his air ticket belonged to Singapore airlines. But the header said it was Emirates. Okay, she knew sometimes airlines would join together to share a flight, and this time, possibly the carrier was Singapore airlines. But Frederick had bought the air ticket through Emirates … even so, it should still be an EKxxx on the ticket.

Third problem: SQ25, according to a Google search, was actually going from New York to Frankfurt on Tuesday.

But Selina had already lost her mind and could not doubt him anymore. 'His travel agent must have made some minor mistake,' she thought. 'Possibly, he is flying from New York to Auckland, but stopping in Frankfurt, which is not shown on the ticket, so he himself didn't know.'

The fourth problem was the biggest …

'Honey,' Selina said, 'the date is wrong. Due to the timezone difference, if you travel on Tuesday morning from New York for a 20-hour flight, you should only arrive on Thursday.'

'You'll have to check it. I'm taking a 20-hour flight to New Zealand. It's a direct flight. I'm not transiting.' Frederick did not understand the problem.

'Yes, but that would mean only 5 hours to come from New York to Auckland? Unless it's referring to New York time for both departure and arrival time?' (Even so, it wouldn't make up 20 hours.)

'Honey. I'm flying Emirates.'

'Okay.'

'My dear, are you home now?' Frederick wanted to change to another topic.

'Yes, I'm at home now.'

'My love, your honey is very nervous. Pray for me. Okay? Pray for my trip. Pray for my work.'

On the day he flew, he talked to her in the morning and showed her photos of his preparing to go to the airport. A photo of his hand holding his US passport *(photo J)*, and another of his pieces of luggage *(photo K)*.

Look at the first photo. Yes, it's an Asian hand, but Selina was under the impression that this hand belongs to a mainland Chinese, not an American Chinese. Although mainland Chinese and American Chinese are the same race, due to the environments that they grew up in, their appearance looks slightly different. Just like Macau Chinese vs mainland Chinese, who look very slightly different. Foreigners can't distinguish, but locals can.

The second photo was also wrong: the suitcases were too small. It wasn't just that you're allowed to bring two big suitcases across America and the Asia Pacific. Frederick's big suitcase was too small for a 3–4 month assignment, especially as it was snowing in New Zealand at that time! If you're going to New Zealand in the winter, you must bring a lot of thick clothes. Of course, if you are very rich, you can buy everything when you arrive in New Zealand.

'My love, what time are you leaving home?'

'I'll leave at 5:45 am.'

Selina thought, 'That's strange. If you leave at 5:45am and drive from your home in Brooklyn to John F. Kennedy International Airport, you would only arrive at the airport at 6:05am. And your flight was at 6:40am!! Shouldn't you arrive at least 1 or 2 hours earlier, to drop luggage and check in????'

Now he was on the flight. 'Honey, I'm nervous. Pray for me.' He sent her a photo of his flight taking off into the sky *(photo L)*. Didn't you have to turn off all electronic devices when the flight was taking off??? Also, business class was at the front of a flight. The wings should be behind you, not in front of you!

*** Scammers can be good at acting like another person, but many make a lot of unexpectedly stupid mistakes in "unimportant" daily life items. Because many scammers have never left their least-developed countries and are only trained in "scam-related" materials. ***

Nevertheless, these topics had nothing to do to any further request for money. So, Selina did not question him. Also, as I've told you, Selina had lost her mind after sending out 70% of her life savings and no longer knew to doubt Frederick.

Next story

After 20 hours, Frederick said he had arrived in New Zealand. He chatted with Selina while he was waiting for his agent to take him to his apartment. It was late at night. Frederick said he was very tired … after taking a business class long flight?

< Selina didn't remember business class being so tiring. >

The next day, Frederick happily showed Selina a cheque that he'd received for his work milestone *(photo M)*. He'd received NZD 4.162 million for the work! Selina was happy for him.

In the afternoon, Frederick texted her, 'Honey, something serious just happened, I've been arrested.'

'Ha? What happened? Are you still able to make contact with me?'

'Hold on, I'll get back to you. Let me try to understand what they want …'

'Honey, do you want me to contact the US embassy for you?'

'No, dear, that would only make it worse.'

Selina was worried for Frederick for the whole day.

The next morning …

Selina asked, 'What reason have they given for restraining you? You're just a normal business person … My love, I'm always with you.'

'Honey, it's very hard to explain right now, but all I can say is that they said I have broken their law and I need to pay a fine. I've been here with them since yesterday and all they are saying is if I want to be released, I need to pay a sum of USD 75,000. If I don't, I'll go to jail. Initially, it was USD 100,000 but I've been able to raise USD 25,000 for them. However, I need to pay the total amount before I'll be released. I never wanted to bother you anymore cos you have been a great help to me all this while, but as it stands now, I have no one to call that can help me. That's why I'm asking you to help, so I can be out of here first. Please, honey, I need you to be my super woman now cos I have no one else other than you.'

'What law do they claim you have broken?'

'They said "money laundry", honey … that NZD 4.162 million was too much and it's against their law.'

'Hahahaha! It doesn't make sense.'

'Honey, this is not funny, coz I have been here with them since yesterday. I had to beg them to allow me to use my phone to chat with you for help. I told them I needed to talk to my wife.'

Selina happened to be familiar with anti-money laundering law (not "money laundry", like Frederick had said). Frederick's stories did not make sense at all. If someone had committed money laundering, would he/she be able to pay a fee and be released?????? Money laundering is a very serious crime!

No such person at our border

Anyway, Selina had already booked her flight to New Zealand when Frederick had said he had arrived in Auckland. She'd fly to meet Frederick tomorrow, and tell him what he should do as a next step, possibly get legal aid for him.

Selina called the New Zealand detention centre. 'Good morning! My fiancé was taken into custody in Auckland yesterday. Can you tell me whether he's being kept in a detention centre or in another department?'

'Sorry, due to privacy reasons, we cannot disclose whether a person is in detention or not.'

Privacy again …

'I'm travelling to Auckland tomorrow … Actually I'm calling from Australia. I've already booked my flight to see my fiancé tomorrow. Can you tell me which detention centre I should go to meet him?'

'Um … What's his surname and first name?'

They said there was no Frederick Chong nor Chong Frederick in the New Zealand detention centre. Selina couldn't believe what she'd heard …

She made a call to New Zealand Immigration. 'Good morning. My fiancé arrived in New Zealand the day before yesterday and said he'd been detained by the police and kept in immigration.'

'Immigration doesn't keep people. What's his surname and first name?'

'Surname: C-H-O-N-G. First name: F-R-E-D-E-R-I-C-K.'

'No. There is no such person at our border. No Frederick Chong nor Chong Frederick. Unless he has another name?'

But that was his name on passport.

Frederick's lie that he was in New Zealand detention was his reason to ask her for money! Selina immediately reported the matter to the Australian police. 'I've sent him SGD 117,600, equivalent to AUD 118,452.80. He says he is now in New Zealand detention and needs more money for bail. But both New Zealand detention and immigration say there is no such person in their country. Probably it's a scam ... or ... maybe it was a misunderstanding ...' Selina still couldn't believe Frederick was fake.

Selina continued, 'Here's his passport details. His surname is ... hang on, his surname and first name are interchanged. It's a fake passport!!!!!'

No victim believes
he/she was scammed.

ALL believe they have
found true love.

THE REAL FREDERICK

Actual geolocation (country) and photo identity

Frederick found in only two days

I was extremely angry. Frederick was fake—which meant my AUD 118,452 was stolen!!!!! Now I had very little money left in my bank account. Two days had passed, but I hadn't heard from the police yet. I screamed crazily at midnight, called the emergency hotline to get attention … these didn't help, of course.

If the police weren't fast enough to catch him, Frederick and his syndicates would spend all my money. I had to do something. How could I get my money back? First, chase the criminal: find out his real geolocation or his real identity.

I was a newbie to this area and had no idea at all how I could capture these.

I thought: Let me first analyse what I have on hand, and the targets that I am trying to achieve …

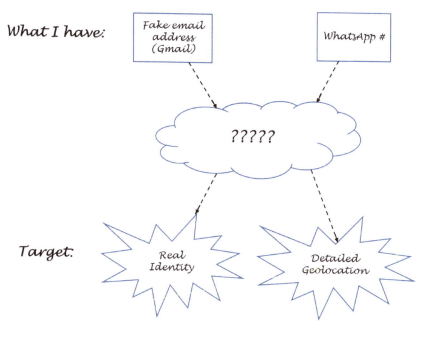

Figure 1 – Selina's analysis.

I looked for key words through the Internet. It took me **only two days** to learn how I could capture his actual geolocation (country and area), do all the configuration and execute the capture!

Here is a screenshot capturing the scammer Frederick's machine information with his IP address on that day/time:

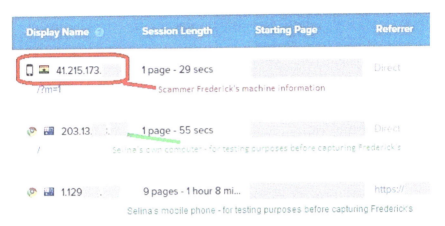

Screenshot a: Frederick's IP address first captured by Selina, three days (2 days + Sunday) after she realised she'd been victimized.

From the lookup, he was currently in Ghana—an African country!

Screenshot b: An IP address lookup revealed that Frederick was currently in an African country—Ghana.

I immediately informed the police of what I'd captured: Scammer Frederick's IP address, country and date captured.

But what did this information mean? To understand it, it's best to compare this with what I had captured earlier on IP addresses from my own mobile phone and my company computer. First, the IP address lookup for my own mobile phone was 1.129.xxx.xxx. According to lookups, this IP address' organisation was my Australian telco.

As for location, one of the IP address / geolocation lookups indicated that my IP address was in Sydney, but another IP address / geolocation lookup website stated that this IP address was in Wollongong. In fact, I was physically in Macquarie Park (20 km away from Sydney, and 89 km from Wollongong), so the IP address / geolocation lookups were referring to the approximate rather than exact geolocation of my Australian telco.

For Frederick (refer to screenshot b), the organization was listed as *Milicom Ghana Limited*. There were three possibilities: a) he was connected to the telco *Milicom Ghana Limited*; b) he was connected to a wifi network that was connected to the telco *Milicom Ghana Limited*; or c) *Milicom Ghana Limited* was not a telco, but a company big enough to have its own IP address, and he was connected to that company's network. If so, then he was physically in that particular company.

I checked on the Internet—*Milicom Ghana Limited* was indeed a telco. So, it had to be either a) or b): Frederick's phone was connected to the Ghana telco *Milicom Ghana Limited*, either through the mobile phone network or through wifi.

As for the city Obuasi, according to a Google search, it was a relatively small town based on mining. It was not too far away from Ghana's capital, Accra—about five hours' drive. In this IP address lookup, region Ashanti, city Obuasi referred to the approximate location of the telco. It might also reveal Frederick's approximate location. But for a developing and relatively small country like Ghana, where the Internet might not be very prevalent, it was possible that the telco might use the same set of DHCP servers to cover all of Ghana. Therefore, the region Ashanti might not be accurate. However, I did believe it was the approximate location, within a five-hour radius of Obuasi. No matter where exactly, he was definitely now physically in Ghana.

The longitude and latitude referred to the approximate location of his Telco *Milicom Ghana Limited*, which was meaningless for my purposes.

Ghana and Nigeria

So, he was certain to be in Ghana. Good, at least he wasn't in Nigeria.

Ghana and Nigeria are neighbouring African countries, about one hour's flight apart. According to my research, Ghana was very different from Nigeria—at the very least, Ghana is much safer to travel to. Looking at the official advice on the Australian government's travel adviser https://smartraveller.gov.au at the time of writing this book, Nigeria had warnings of *"Do not travel"* or *"Re-consider your need to travel"* (the two worst rankings). Ghana had only *"Exercise normal safety precautions"* (the best ranking). Even the famous Mr Kofi Annan, the seventh Secretary General of the United Nations, had grown up in Ghana and graduated from a university there. He was a reputable man considered to have contributed a lot towards peace in the world.

Nigeria and Ghana both have many romance scammers. Some romance-scam criminal groups in these countries are even connected. They are very hard to catch. One of the obvious reasons: corruption. Some government officers are said to receive death threats if they attempt to arrest local Internet romance scammers. However, it's said that the United States has done a lot to help Nigerian police catch their Internet romance scammers. Another reason is poverty. I don't mean criminals commit the crime because they are poor (some criminals in these countries are quite rich), but because those countries are still struggling to feed the whole community with basic necessities. How can you expect their governments to allocate a lot of resources to catch criminals who attack foreign countries?

According to research, the layouts of romance scams from different countries are slightly different. Nigeria is considered to have the most romance scammers in the world, while Ghana is considered second. But Ghana scammers frequently create and execute forged documents, including fake passports and fake banking documents. Another difference is that Nigerian scammers mainly use male scammers to fake both male and female dating profiles. They do this by playing video tapes of male/female voices of 'Hello … Hello …', pretending the phone reception is terrible and getting you to chat with them by texting instead of phone calls. Ghana has similar amounts of both male or female romance scammers. According to the news, romance scammers usually do not have good command of English and rely on pre-written scripts to talk to victims. However, in Frederick's case, his command of English was comparable to my own, a Macau immigrant to Australia who'd studied English from two years old. He also talked to me a lot on phones. Criminals' scamming skills are improving!

Wok?? Walk?? What?????

Now I remembered, Frederick previously said to me, 'Selina, your English pronunciation of the word w-o-r-k "work" is not correct. It should be "wok". You should say, I'm going to "wok" today.'

I said, 'Wok?? Walk?? What???? Hey, can it possibly be a matter of American accents vs UK accents? But I'm sure everyone says "work" … I occasionally work with people from the US. I'm sure they all pronounce it "work".'

Frederick confidently said, 'No. It should be "wok".'

Hearing Frederick so confident that he challenged the English of an Australian lady, I didn't question him further and believed he was indeed from the United States. But now I double-checked the pronunciation on the online Cambridge dictionary, I found the American pronunciation is "work".

So, a stupid thing: Frederick, an uneducated scammer from Ghana, thought that Australia was an Asian country (due to its close geolocation to Asia). He challenged Australian Chinese Selina about her English pronunciation. Selina saw his impressive confidence and didn't challenge him back.

Stupid! Stupid! Both were stupid!

Saturdays and Sundays

Now I recalled, when I first knew Frederick, I was excited about Saturdays and Sundays—I thought he would have more time to chat with me on the weekends.

'My love, I worked a full day yesterday. Today, I'm tired. I'm staying at home to watch soccer. You enjoy yourself, okay?' This ended up the typical Frederick weekend conversation.

I myself also sometimes play soccer; but I love playing it, not watching it. Frederick said he loved soccer. He always watched soccer on the weekend, but I'd never heard him say he went to play soccer. Except for an occasional few hours, he spent the FULL DAY every weekend concentrated on watching soccer, and not much time talking to me. Shouldn't you spend more time talking to your lover on weekends?

Now I understand, the young scammer, Frederick, needed to hang out with his gang on weekends!

Second round photo search—the real Frederick

Seven days had passed since I reported the case to the police, so I called to see how the case was going.

'We haven't yet decided whether or not to look into your case.'

'What? But the IP address and actual country was captured, and his passport was confirmed to be fake. It's a certain case of fraud. You still haven't decided whether to look into the case or not???'

Last year, I lost my wallet in the city. The police investigated the case and called me back in three days about their findings in regard to the AUD 100 lost. This time, I lost AUD 118,452, and the police hadn't even decided whether or not to look at it after one week. The volume of romance scam was just too high for the Australian police to take that long deciding whether to even accept a case or not. It might be reasonable from a government resource allocation perspective, but it causes massive pain to victims, especially as there are so many victims.

I couldn't just wait for everything from the police. I needed to find out as much as I could. 'So, whose face is the man I knew as "Frederick"? The man whom I thought I was going to marry?'

I did a second round of searches on Google. Frederick had provided a total of 14 photos and two videos of "himself". I searched his photos one by one. Twelve photos were searched—no hits at all.

'Does that mean I'll never know who this man actually is—the man that I thought I was going to marry? God, my merciful Lord, please help. I hope I'll learn who he is. I hope I can say something to the real person, the person whom I thought I was going to marry.'

I felt hopeless. Now it was the last photo—"Frederick" with his dog. I thought, 'It's not going to hit. It's just a dog photo.'

Search result: Two hits!!

- Twitter – Franco Yeung – more than a thousand followers?
- Facebook – Franco Yeung

Here is Franco Yeung's background: he belongs to the Democratic party in Los Angeles and works in the Mayor's Office. He was born in Los Angeles, grew up in Los Angeles, but studied in New York for some time.

No wonder Frederick said his father was a politician in Los Angeles—it was in reference to the real "Frederick"—Franco Yeung!

Looking at Franco's photos in Facebook—the real Franco seems more charming than the fake Frederick. Well, I don't mean the real Franco is charming; I mean, "more" charming than the fake person. The real Franco looks more sunny, more lively, while the fake Frederick always feels a little bit on the dark side. I don't know why.

I read through the entirety of Franco Yeung's Facebook, his posts and photos from the present back until he was born. About 70% of the photos that Frederick had sent me were found in Franco's Facebook.

Photo A: The real Franco was wearing protection glasses and a safety hat, because this politician was having a hard hat tour to a War Memorial Veterans' Building that was under renovation.

Photo C: My sense was correct: it was indeed a vineyard. Franco was in a vineyard but Frederick had said he was in a conference meeting.

Photos B and D were also in Franco's Facebook.

Oh my God! Frederick's passport photo (*Photo H*)! Franco's Facebook has a description of the photo: *'I'm pretty sure there's a lot more to life than being really, really ridiculously good-looking. And I plan on finding out what that is.'*—Franco thought himself very good-looking when he took that photo. Argh!! Franco, why did you take that kind of photo????? Do you know this photo lost me a lot of my money!!! Focusing on the hair, the photoshop editing by the criminal was not perfect. Some tiny hairs were cut away, but that wasn't important for the purpose of producing a fake passport.

And the photo in Frederick's Meetup.com profile: the original photo was from Franco's campaign with his helpers to call and remind people to vote for him. The parts of the original photos showing election materials had been cut out of Frederick's version.

Looking at other photos in Franco's Facebook, there were a lot of photos on election day with his supporters. Franco with groups of supporters! And, Franco with *Hillary Clinton*?? In another photo, he was surrounded by 12 Chinatown beauty pageant contestants. Haha! So funny!

This Franco loves taking photos, too much. Makes it easy for criminals to exploit. But as he is a politician, he has to release a lot of his photos. He doesn't seem to be senior enough to get public attention outside the United States; perhaps, not even outside Los Angeles. So, victims wouldn't be able to tell who he was.

Ha, it looks like this real Franco is quite a funny person. But, not my style, I wouldn't love him, even if I knew the real Franco.

Another victim?

So, 70% of Frederick's photos were found in Franco's Facebook. What about the remaining 30%? What about his two personal videos? Also, some of the photos in Franco's Facebook were exploitable, but were not taken by the criminal. Why? Because the criminal didn't get his photos from Facebook. The criminal pretended to be a beautiful woman, possibly on Meetup. (I don't think this politician Franco would go for online dating.) She made Franco send "her" his photos and personal videos (video 1 and 2). They captured these photos and videos and used his face to create a fake profile on Meetup.com, and scammed women!

Yes, according to Facebook, this Franco is indeed single.

Franco, please!!!! Do you know how much money I lost because of your video 2???

Now I understand why Frederick asked me to send him more photos—he wanted to use my face to create a new fake online dating profile! Luckily, I rarely take photos and those in his hands should be insufficient for this purpose.

* Disclaimer: Franco is NOT actually from Los Angeles. We used "Los Angeles" in this book to protect his identity.

Fake third-party email address

Frederick is certainly a scammer. The general advice is to stop talking to a scammer. But he has stolen so much money from me. If I stop talking to him, the police and myself can miss vital clues on how to catch him (and how to get my money back). Why should I kiss my money goodbye!!!???

I will pretend I don't know he is a fake. If so … what will I say to him?

I shouted at him, 'Hey, honey, your USD 113,000 still hasn't arrived!!!!! Can you chase it up with your bank????'

'Honey, I'm in custody now. I can't use my phone freely. I had to beg the police to let me talk to you, my wife.'

'Then authorise me to chase my USD 113,000 on your behalf!'

After a few minutes, Frederick got back to me. 'Here is my banking agent's email: USA-federal-reserve-bank@USA.com.'

Frederick, you are a full-time actor. Can't you show some professionalism?? This email address is obviously fake! USA.com is a company. A federal reserve bank is a government organization and should go with .gov or .org, not .com! Um … but let me email it to see what will come up. Who knows? Perhaps it'll give me a little clue about this criminal group.

I emailed the illegitimate email address, but no reply. Apparently, it was already closed by USA.com, as it's obviously illegitimate.

Controlling Frederick's mind

'Honey, your banking agent's email address doesn't work,' I said.

'Okay, I'll sort it out when I get out of here. Honey, have you sent the money to bail me out yet?'

'My love, borrowing money takes time. Don't stress me, ok?' I said to Frederick.

Now, I pretended I was borrowing money for bail to release Frederick from New Zealand custody, as he requested. Frederick wouldn't get suspicious, because romance scammers often get their victims into big loans to feed them. They always want to get as much money as possible. Then they can buy fancy cars, go to expensive top hotels and buy gifts for girls—leaving their victims bankrupt. Victims are forced to sell their homes and are fired by their employers. This is very common.

I acted angrily. 'Honey, you were calling me 10 times a day for the last few days, more than any time since we met. You borrowed USD 113,000 from me and the money hasn't been returned, and now you're stressing me out about paying your bail, as if I owe you money? I'm not happy!'

But this uncivilized Frederick had difficulty in controlling himself. He was rushing to get more money to buy his new fantasy—maybe diamonds for new girlfriends? He continued to harass me.

I blamed him. 'What the hell is that? I've already told you—I'm waiting for the loan to bail you out. Have you even heard what I said? Why am I talking to you? You just don't listen. And I tell you what, if you continue to blame me one single more time, I will be very happy to leave you in jail for the rest of your life.'

'I can tell you don't love me much!'

'Honey, you don't understand women? A woman only loves you if you love her.'

Frederick, think about it: getting money late is better than never.

Now, Frederick could only continue to wait for me. He mustn't offend me anymore, or he'd never get more money from me … or so he believed. He'd better go back to continuing his love songs. From then, I created trouble for him by manipulating his poor English and making up a few virtual stories to confuse him …

Selina the actress: the romance continues …

'Honey, you know the reason why I need your help? It's because I love you and I don't want to lose you,' Frederick said.

'♡ My love, I'm going to cook dinner now. Talk later. Have a good sleep ☆ ☾,' I said.

Frederick replied, 'Honey, dream of Frederick. Us, together. You are my heart.'

'☆'

'My love, pray for our marriage. It's going to be great.'

'I know, my love. ♡'

'Loving you is a battle. I won't surrender.'

'♡ I won't surrender either,' I said.

Listening to Frederick's love songs, it was hard for me to believe he was really fake. But with his actual physical location captured and the real Franco's Facebook in front of me, what could I say?

IP ADDRESS – OVERVIEW

In cybercrime, we frequently talk about IP addresses. Here is an overview for your understanding:

1) Format: IP address = xxx.xxx.xxx.xxx, where xxx is a number 0 to 255.

2) An IP address is **unique, but shared**. In the picture below, mobile devices A, B, C and E are all behind Telco A. When capturing IP address, all will be captured as 14.100.125.80.

3) An IP address is **dynamic**. For example, in the morning, mobile A is connected to its mobile network, and its IP address is 14.100.125.80. In the afternoon, the owner of mobile A goes back to his office company C and uses the wifi. Now, the IP address of mobile A changes to 155.4.7.8.

   Further, even if you are always connected to your mobile network, when you move from one city to another, you will probably connect to a different router and hence have a different IP address.

4) Behind the router, they allocate you with a unique "Internal IP address", ranging from 0.0.0.0 to 255.255.255.255. This is not usually captured unless you're using a more professional tool. And this information is not usually very useful as it is dynamic: today, they assign you with a certain internal IP address, tomorrow they assign you with another.

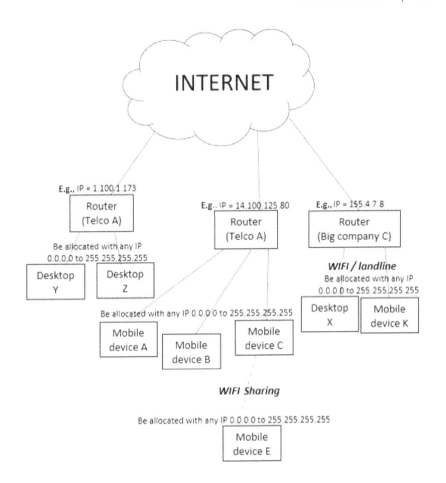

Figure 2 – IP address / DHCP overview.

The next important question is, can IP addresses be fake?

When you attempt to "visit a website" (or other Internet applications), effectively you are telling them, 'I want to see the contents of your website. Can you please send them to me?' If you fake your IP address, how do they deliver information to you?

Therefore, to appear as a "fake" IP address, it is possible to first route to another place before going to the Internet. But this usually still has a trace and has logistic considerations for criminals.

Therefore, most of the time, capturing IP address gives you knowledge on a criminal's geolocation (country, area), or at least, tells you where to trace from; but it is not sufficient to know who he/she is.

As of the time of writing, it is believed that the majority of Internet romance scammers do not even attempt to fake their IP addresses. The most important element of an Internet romance scam is not technology, but lies and acting. The people committing these crimes are not smarter than you, they are only full-time liars.

POLICE

Fake passport? I care, but I can't care ...

Useful booklets—only found in police stations

Two weeks after I reported my case to the police, I received a call from Inspector Haden, from the NSW police. Haden invited me to come to the police station for a meeting.

While waiting for Inspector Haden in the reception area of the police station, I saw the *Little Black Book of Scams*. The book was published by the government and had useful information about all types of scams ... but I had only seen it distributed in a police station, not elsewhere. Therefore, probably you will only know that book after you are confirmed to have lost a fortune in scams and go to a police station.

Frederick's fake passport

Inspector Haden smiled relaxingly in the whole conversation. Probably, he wanted me to relax. 'What you received was a low-quality fake passport. Look, this one is the original passport that he amended.'

I looked at it. 'I don't understand?'

'This is the original one that the scammer copied from. I got it from the web.'

'But why do you say it is copied from this one and not another one?'

At the end of the conversation, I eventually understood he was referring to the passport owner's signature, which was definitely not Frederick's, but a woman's name. *(Refer to the signature in Photo E)*

'OMG! I thought that was a signature from a US government official!'

It was really a ridiculous mistake by the forged document creator, so ridiculous that I could not even interpret that it was meant to be a passport owner's signature. I should have checked my own passport so that I knew that passports needed to have a passport owner's signature. I'd thought passports from different countries could be different, so I hadn't compared it with my own passport.

A real Frederick Chong in Africa vs a fake Frederick Chong in Africa vs a real Franco Yeung with Frederick's face

Now, Haden showed me a real "Frederick Chong" in an African country. I said, 'No, there are a few Frederick Chongs in the world, but it's a coincidence. They are not related to this case. Chong is a real Cantonese Chinese surname, which happens to also be a surname in Africa. The criminals just randomly chose the name "Frederick Chong", not to pretend to be any real Frederick Chong. Possibly they chose this name because the spelling is similar to the real person in the photos, "Franco".' Then I showed Haden the real Franco Yeung's Facebook.

'You've found him! Good!' said Haden.

'I'll inform Franco about his photos being stolen and used for fake online dating profiles. Hopefully he'll ask the US police for help to catch the thieves.'

'Haha, if I were him, I wouldn't call the US police—it's a shame he as a politician got scammed.'

'If he doesn't call the US police, then this fake US passport with his face will continue to flow around the world, until people recognise his face as a scammer, not a politician. His political life will be damaged.'

'Okay, then you try to contact Franco.'

Suspicious but no evidence.
What if he was real and honest?

I said, 'I've done a lot of checking on whether this Frederick was real or not. I also contacted JP Morgan Chase to check whether the banking document was real or fake and whether Frederick was indeed their customer or not. However, they were unwilling to disclose whether the banking document was real or fake, due to privacy reasons. I felt totally helpless at that time. I thought, what if the banking document was real and I was holding the funds? Then Frederick'd fail his project and lose everything because he trusted me; and I'd lose the family that was to belong to me. I thought, I'd spent so much effort to prove Frederick was fake, and I failed; so I decided to assume he and his documents were real.'

'I see. Selina, it's unfortunate that you fell victim.'

'It's not unfortunate. It's totally avoidable. As you say, this is an everyday crime. Why has the government never told us what to check? How on earth would I know romance scammers are usually from African countries? If I knew that, I would have captured his actual country from day 1. How on earth would I know romance scammers are creating fake passports and fake banking documents? I know these can be faked easily, but I know it is a much more serious crime than a confidence fraud, so I didn't expect romance scammers would dare to commit it. How on earth would I know this kind of crime almost always has zero money recovery? If I knew I was not protected by law, I wouldn't even have considered sending out the first lot of funds. How on earth would I know to search through all his photos? If the crime is so common, why has the government done so little to tell the public how to avoid these scams? And once we fall victim, governments say they don't have sufficient resources to look at it!'

'It's been in Scamwatch.'

'Who knows about Scamwatch? No one knows about it. My friends don't know, the banks don't know. Only government agencies know about it. I first heard about Scamwatch after falling victim.

What the hell is the use of this secret website? Also, this *Little black book of scams*, I'd never seen it in my life, only in the police station after I was confirmed as victimized. What's the use?????'

Obviously, it was for a different department, not the police, to do public education about scams. I would send feedback/suggestions to that government department later.

Police have limited power, but your case won't be escalated

Haden said, 'Now, about your case, only the federal police have the power to catch overseas scammers. We state police can attempt to escalate your case for you, but they probably won't look into it. This type of scam is an everyday crime in Australia now. Internet romance scams are sophisticated and require a lot of resources to investigate. The monetary loss in your case is quite large, but probably the federal police still won't look at it.'

*** These rules are not country-specific. Related rules in developed countries are more or less the same. Please check with your government for the most accurate and latest information.

I'll do the work

'What if I do the technical work to find the scammer? I'm an IT consultant. I understand the federal police don't have the resources, but I do.'

'Try your best, Selina.'

'I will. Actually, I'm new to this area. But he stole too much money from me. I must do everything I can.'

'So, you are not an expert in this area?'

'No. I'm a financial IT consultant. But it shouldn't be too difficult for us IT consultants to pick up new IT skills. It'll take some time but it's do-able.'

Franco with Frederick's face?
Or Frederick with Franco's face?

Leaving the police station, the first thing I did was to call Franco Yeung in California. It was very easy to find out his direct line as his position was to liaise with the public. Actually, I had been trying to call him for a few days, but it happened to be an election day in his area so he was probably away from his office—no one answered.

I called him again and left him a message, telling him I was an Australian Chinese IT consultant, calling to inform him about a cybercrime against him, hoping he would call me back.

Listening to his voice mail, his voice was much more normal than the fake Frederick. The real Franco did not have an unusual English accent, just a normal American-born Chinese speaking normal English calmly and clearly. I was glad that I could hear the real person's voice. I was hoping to talk to him—I confess I was still attached to something about this person, whom I'd thought I was to marry soon.

As Haden expected, Franco never called me back. As for me, I was looking at Frederick's actual geolocation, and his photos in the real Franco's Facebook and Twitter. Two weeks later, my feelings about Frederick and Franco vanished. I no longer missed either of them.

Luckily and unluckily

Selina felt frustrated: As the police said, this kind of crime happens every day, they've accepted my case, but were unlikely to do anything about it.

Selina felt graceful: At least I've got to the truth so quickly. According to the news, many victims don't even know whether their online lovers are real or fake for more than a year after reporting their cases to the police or the cybercrime reporting authority.

Selina felt humble: It was me who had offended God during the year. I have reduced my one-tenth donation to the church, which is commanded in the Bible. Since I'd graduated, I'd been strictly obeying it. But I've reduced it recently—I was angry with God when Jason went with the actress.

The Bible considers this equivalent to having stolen God's money. That's why I've now had my money stolen—fair enough! I'm happy to know God is real!

Selina felt lucky: At least I'd not been conned into drug trafficking or money laundering, which would have put me in jail.

Selina felt glad: So, the Frederick was fake. God has not arranged a replacement for Jason, so maybe Jason would still come back one day?

Selina felt relieved: I'm clever and I'd been victimized by an idiot in a romance scam, then Jason can also have been scammed by a fresh graduate for his money and a permanent Australian visa! The actress will leave sooner or later!

Selina felt insulted: You stupid, low-level scammer, rubbish of the rubbish in society! I have most of my money stolen by a rat like you?

Selina felt angry: You stupid rubbish, committing a serious cybercrime using a fake passport and fake banking documents against a top-tier Australian IT consultant? You think you can safely walk away? I'm going to put you in jail with my very own hands!

Now, Selina's anger turned into energy. In the next few months, she would go through the most hard-working days of her life.

Timeline

6 July (Friday): Selina's case was reported to the **Australian police**.

8 July (Sunday): Selina's case was reported to the **Singapore police**, Jurong division (to which bank account owner Ling Tien Tien's address, *Cha Chu Kang,* belonged).

A few weeks later, the Singapore police informed her that they required Interpol to send through the information for them to investigate.

In Australia, Interpol was under the federal police. That means the case would only be looked at by Singapore if her case was escalated to Interpol or the federal police.

Selina reported her case to the **Ghana police** through emails three times—ALL were ignored.

CASE PRIORITISATION BY FEDERAL POLICE

No matter which country, local police generally do not have the power to catch overseas criminals. That requires the federal police or Interpol, whose primary responsibility is to investigate criminal offences against the country. Generally, they would not have the resources to investigate all reports by individuals.

As of the time of writing of this book, the federal police website explained their Case Categorisation and Prioritisation Model. In terms of priority, drugs at the border and family law, among others, should receive immediate attention. In terms of impact, terrorism, national security, real threats to life and harming of Australians overseas, child sex offences and exploitation with immediate risk, cybercrime targeting national infrastructure, economic crime affecting whole of government agencies or valued at more than AUD 5 million, human trafficking, large scale identity theft—these are considered very high impact.

It makes sense! This is what the national police should do—protect the nation, protect people's lives and safety.

Economic crime affecting government agencies within a region or valued at more than AUD 0.25 million is only considered medium impact.

Personal nuisance: low impact. Cases with little likelihood of success are also classified as low impact.

They also consider other factors such as the resources required to investigate the case, the values involved and the impact on the client.

In Internet romance scams, most are initialised by scammers located in third-world countries. Uncivilized criminals gain easy money from you. Then they easily spend all the money on fancy cars, expensive hotels and diamonds to get girls. When they use up all the money, they sell those fancy cars and diamonds at very cheap prices to get food and toilet paper (if they use it). That's why the likelihood of recovering money by catching these scammers is almost zero. In other words, making a huge effort to catch the scammers probably won't bring any help to existing victims.

If the romance scam was run by international criminal groups, there is still a chance some money is left with more civilized criminals in developed countries. These criminals at least may not spend all the money in one go. Even so, it usually requires a lot of resources and a lot of international cooperation for police to catch them.

Now you understand why most Internet romance scams aren't escalated.

However, no single element of the Case Categorisation and Prioritisation Model is considered in isolation. Instead, federal police consider a combination of the model's impact and priority ratings. This is not based on a mathematical formula and does not supplant the discretion of decision makers.

* Disclaimer: We do not have a relationship with any police force. The above information is our understanding after reading the federal police website and related news. Please refer to your country's federal police website for the most accurate and latest information.

We wrote this section so that you'll understand why it's very hard to catch scammers, even if you lost millions of dollars. So, please, do not even pay a cent.

IT DETECTIVE

What if the victim is a hacker???

The financial consultant

I sat down to reassess my financial situation. Originally, that year, I was supposed to pay about AUD 25,000 in tax to the Australian Tax Office. Now, I could claim a loss of AUD 118,452 due to theft, quoting my police event number, then I didn't need to pay a cent of tax! Apparently, there was also some leftover for me to deduct from my tax for next year too. So, the net loss reduced to AUD 90,000–93,000.

Thinking about the following fact further eased my turbulent feelings about losing money in a scam: I didn't buy a property a few years ago, and Sydney's housing market has gone up a lot. The net loss of not owning a property a few years earlier was more than AUD 200,000. That means I'd lost this AUD 200,000 for, again, nothing.

So, in comparison to the loss in housing market, losing AUD 90,000 in a scam was not too bad.

Now, I felt better. I got calm.

The IT detective

Let me focus on tracing the thief. This was the plan I came up with:

First, I kept the scammer online with me. I didn't want to lose track of the thief who had stolen a fortune from me. There were also a few more reasons for this: i) if he was spending his effort and concentration on entertaining me, then he'd have less time and concentration to scam other people; ii) I may need his co-operation when I later find out how to capture his real identity and geo-details; and iii) I prayed to God, to enquire whether I should continue to keep him online or not, and I heard the answer "yes" twice, so I had to do it.

Keeping him online caused me inconvenience, but I had to do it.

Second, I researched Ghana, to learn about the country's background. I also researched "Ghana Scammers", "Romance scam Ghana", and "Ghana Scams" to understand the kind of people that have possibly committed this crime, their culture, their government's attitude towards this crime, and his educational background, among other things (this analysis was presented in Chapter 6).

Third, I re-visited the data captured about his IP address. He was in Ghana, and his telco was *Millicom Ghana Limited*. The data also revealed that he was using Android, and a mobile phone, not a computer. This was good news. Android was known to have a lot of security holes (or maybe it had been improved?) But the bad news: he was not using a computer, which meant this object could move!

And he was in Ghana … According to the news, romance scammers in Ghana are likely to be living in nothing more than a slum. Considering the latest Android version and the background of this poor Frederick, I estimated that he was using Android 6 or similar. Although he had stolen my money, I didn't think he would buy a new phone for the purposes of Internet romance scams. He might have had a primary phone for his "usual" purposes, and this Android phone was only a secondary phone for romance scams. So, he probably wouldn't have bothered to get the latest technology for this criminal phone.

Therefore, I estimated he was using around an Android 6. I'd always been an iPhone user; I'd never used Android. So, I immediately ordered an Android 6 mobile phone to test my systems against it. I bought it online, so it took a few days to arrive.

In the meantime, I researched the systems that could serve my purposes. But what were my purposes? Looking back to figure 1, the targets "real identity" and "detailed geolocation" were too generic. I needed to break down the targets into smaller, concrete pieces. Also, I needed to add the facts (e.g., Android, Ghana) that I'd already found:

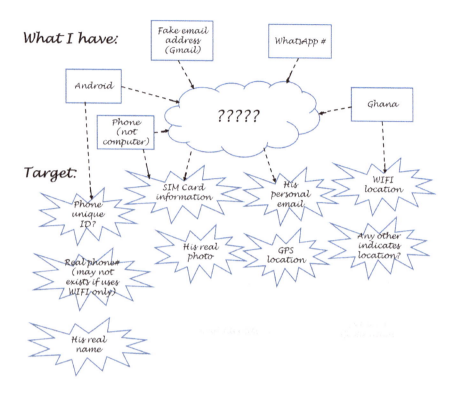

Figure 3 – Selina's analysis (broken down into smaller targets).

Much better now.

I applied my usual IT project methodology: 1) define the scope/ targets, 2) select the appropriate system(s), 3) obtain and build the system, and possibly do some programming, 4) do internal testing and 5) apply this in the real environment—Frederick's machine.

I had to be quick. Scammers in Ghana and Nigeria are idiots. They earn easy money and spend it all quickly, without using their brains. Unless they are controlled by international criminal groups, in which case most of the money may stay with the more civilized criminals who know how to keep the money.

Building two professional IT systems in only 1.5 months

Given he was using Android, I spent a few days researching and selected two possible systems. I downloaded system A, installed it on my company computer. (Sorry, boss, but I knew you wouldn't mind as the computer did have much space left at that moment. I would remove it later.) I needed to do some Java programming as well, so I borrowed a few books from the public library.

Five days later, system A was fully built and I'd started doing some programming. But when it came to testing, it did not behave as I desired.

System A – FAIL!

So, I decided to use system B instead. System B was an even more professional system. The advantage of system B was that almost everything was built-in, but configuring the system alone was complex enough. I remembered when I was in university, my final year project was a simplified version of a similar system. If I hadn't had two strong classmates in the same project group, I wouldn't have been able to graduate: I simply didn't understand how to use it! I don't remember having successfully completed any tasks at all!

But now, I was a senior IT consultant. Even if I was brand new to this system, it was not too difficult for me to build it. And the point was, my only target was to achieve my particular purpose, not becoming an expert in all aspects. Believe me, this is the life of an IT consultant. Today, your boss gives you a new system to study. Two weeks later, you're teaching your colleagues how to use it. Two more weeks later, the company presents you to their clients as an expert on that system.

I took out my seven-year-old personal computer and partitioned it as dual-boot for Windows and system B. I built, and re-built, and re-built, and re-re-re-re-re-re-re-re-re-re-re-re-re-built it, and added two additional external tools. I tested it against my new Android 6 phone, and also tested it against my company computer and my iPhone. (What if he uses a computer to connect next time? Better to test it on both an Android phone and a computer.)

System B – PASS! My system was working!

It took me seven weeks to setup the entire system and tools. It costed me a total of AUD 13.10 = AUD 10 (for an external tool) + AUD 2.10 + AUD 1 (for transport to two public libraries to borrow books). But it took a lot of effort—I was working day and night, even Saturdays. I happened to have a business trip to Singapore. During the day I worked for my company, but every evening after work, I immediately went back to the hotel and did all the system configuration in the beautiful Singapore harbour view hotel club lounge till late at night. Every evening when I arrived, the hotel always offered me with a full table of delicious tapas, cakes and a couple of cocktails—all included in the room charge, luckily. Thanks boss! I often overate, as I kept eating when I did system configuration for hours every night, and the food was really delicious!

Sitting there for hours every night, everyone in the hotel recognized me! A few retiree hotel guests saw me and said with a smile, 'Signorina, don't work too hard.'

Who is a hacker? Frederick or Selina?

Final step: I needed to connect Frederick's machine to my computer. I sent him a fake website, which was actually hosted by my computer—the web server and webpages were all run on my personal computer—system B. I made up some stories to ask Frederick to visit my fake website. Once Frederick visited my website, many scripts were run automatically to capture his information: his phone brand, model, screen size and connection method.

From here, I captured two more IP addresses from him—now he was in Nigeria, connected through wifi. He was holding an Infinix phone—a Nigerian brand, available in both Nigeria and Ghana. Bingo! His phone was indeed an Android 6.0—my guess was correct! His phone was the same Android version as the one I was holding in my hand, the one that I'd just bought to test the behaviour of his phone!

(Almost all Internet romance scammers know that clicking a URL can reveal their actual geolocation. But because they are faking being in love with you, they can't always say, 'I don't want to click your links, I don't want to visit your websites.' They also can't use technical problems as an excuse not to click your URL. Because, technically, it is not quite possible that he can text you online using an encrypted application like Whatsapp, but be unable to visit your website. If he can talk to you through Whatsapp but says he cannot click your link, then he is lying.)

The good news was that it was certain Frederick had been across Ghana to Nigeria in the past seven weeks—Ghana's immigration department must have his record. But it also raised a new question: was Frederick a Ghanaian or a Nigerian?

First, according to the data, his first Nigerian connection was certainly through wifi—probably, he was not in his own country and therefore needed to use wifi. Second, looking at the time he went to sleep (went offline), I noticed he had always been sleeping at 4am Ghana time, but these one to two weeks, he was sleeping earlier than usual, at 3am Ghana time. This was because Nigeria was one hour ahead of Ghana! He sleeps at 4am local time: Nigeria 4am = Ghana 3am.

Therefore, he was very likely a Ghanaian, currently in Nigeria. And he was very likely to have travelled from Ghana to Nigeria between 7 to 14 days ago.

CRIMINAL:	FREDERICK CHONG / FEDERICK CHONG (FAKE NAME)
REAL NAME:	UNKNOWN
NATIONALITY:	GHANAIAN
AGE:	ABOUT 20 YEARS

(HE DOESN'T UNDERSTAND WOMEN. SURE, MEN NEVER UNDERSTAND WOMEN, BUT YOUNG MEN MISUNDERSTAND IN A DIFFERENT WAY. ALSO, YOUNG MEN ARE MORE LIKELY TO GO TO SLEEP AS LATE AS 4AM.)

EDUCATION LEVEL:	HIGH SCHOOL OR SIMILAR

(HIS ENGLISH WAS GOOD ENOUGH TO CONCLUDE HE HAD HIGH SCHOOL LEVEL; BUT HIS OVERALL KNOWLEDGE WAS NOT SUFFICIENT TO BE A UNIVERSITY GRADUATE.)

ENGLISH LEVEL:	GOOD, BUT OBVIOUSLY NOT NATIVE
BACKGROUND:	NEVER STUDIED IN DEVELOPED COUNTRIES
COUNTRIES VISITED:	NIGERIA, FRANCE (POSSIBLY), TURKEY (POSSIBLY)

HE WAS LIKELY TO HAVE VISITED FRANCE AND TURKEY, AS HE SPECIFICALLY MENTIONED HE VISITED THESE TWO COUNTRIES IN HIS STORY. IF HE HAD NEVER BEEN THERE, VICTIMS MIGHT EASILY CHALLENGE HIS LACK OF KNOWLEDGE.

It was still not sufficient to know who he exactly was. I wanted a) his detailed geolocation, and/or b) his real identity, such as his real name or Ghanaian phone number. I probably needed to further configure my system, or add additional external software, or do some programming.

*Note: as of today, the above system B is not used in services provided by Alpaca Consulting IT Pty Ltd. The tool in Chapter 6 is good enough to capture what you need to identify romance scams. *

Do it legally

Hijacking his phone or computer would not be difficult. What about commanding his phone to send me a text message, so that I get his real Ghanaian phone number? Or commanding his phone to take a photo of him, and send it to me? Maybe I should ask his phone to turn on his GPS and send me his detailed GPS location? Or his wifi geolocation? I might even tell his phone to send me his address book, so that his syndicates could be identified. What about sending me his Whatsapp database for decryption?

But would it be legal for me to do these things? I wasn't going to risk it if I wasn't certain. Obviously, I didn't want to get myself into trouble for Frederick—he's just an underground creature. Wasn't worth it. My tool was strong enough to do a lot, but I had to be certain it was legal before doing anything further.

Doing the technical work would not be very difficult, but it was more difficult to gauge the boundary between what was legal and what was illegal. Well, there are so many new technologies all the time, so it is hard for the law to specify rules for each of them. Some legal documents in Australia say it depends on your intention and on which state you belong to. According to these, as long as I don't alter his data, it should be fine. And, according to the news, there had been no case law on victims being accused of hacking a criminal's system.

But were these true or not? I had to be certain before I did anything further.

Can be captured, but not useful

Other than the legal aspect, there are other things to consider. First, obviously, is do-ability. Some software or spyware requires you to have physical access to the target's machine at least once to install it. I obviously did not have this access.

Second is capturability. There are unique IDs to identify a particular computer or phone; for example, IMEI, UUID, IMSI, Android ID and MAC addresses. It is said that there is a so-called "computer fingerprint" as well.

In theory, many things can be captured by running appropriate scripts, but only some can be captured by simple Internet languages such as Javascript. Many require certain types of programming languages, and those languages can only be run if the target has installed the software. That means it would, again, require me to either install it in the target or use a virus to run it in the target. Creating a virus is illegal, so I wasn't going to do that.

Third, for those items that can easily be captured by simple Internet languages like Javascript, are they usually transmitted? What I mean is, as per figure 2, each machine would first go through the router of the telco Internet provider before going out to the Internet. Would the telco be able to see this item? For example, MAC address is not transmitted, while IMSI is. That means, to my understanding, your telco would have a record of your IMSI, but no record of your MAC address. Telco can easily trace the current location of a target machine using IMSI, but not MAC address. Therefore, if I could capture IMSI, it would be very useful, as the telco could identify where the machine currently was; but if I capture MAC address, that wouldn't be useful, as the telco has no information about it—no one has.

Fourth, nullable and fakeable: some unique machine identifiers, interestingly, can be null. For example, Android_ID can be null, and can even be altered. IMEI is always unique, but many devices don't have IMEI.

Maybe the police or other professional IT investigators have better solutions than mine. After all, I'm a financial IT specialist, a newbie to tracing criminals. The above findings took me months of study. But the police surely have more legal power to do things that IT professionals cannot do legally. For example, only the police have power to hack into SS7; it's illegal for the public to hack into SS7. And the police probably have better tools to trace cybercriminals, but it still takes significant effort. With the current very high volume of Internet romance scams (together with other cybercrimes), the police probably are not able to look into the details for each romance scam case.

CRITICAL THINKING: SPYWARE

Some spyware claims to be 100% legal to use, especially on your children, husband or wife. One of the obvious reasons is for safety: you want to know where your children are. If they are lost, with the spyware, you can easily find them. You also want to be sure they aren't browsing harmful websites or adult materials. And you may even want to monitor their Internet conversations to ensure they are not exposed to crime.

Same as for a husband or a wife. You want to know their whereabouts in case of any accident or if they come home late, that they weren't attacked or kidnapped or something like that. But using spyware on a spouse has another function: to spy on them in case of any cheating. It is said that spyware has contributed to evidence in many spousal cheating cases in court.

Now, Frederick claims that he is my husband-to-be. Does that mean I can legally install spyware on his phone and his computer??

(We raised this topic for critical thinking only. If you want to do this, please first consult your legal adviser.)

HOW TO SCAM
A SCAMMER?

You want to brainwash me?
Let me brainwash you.

Learning pianoforte may not necessary make one a great pianist, but from that, one learns how to be influential, how to express virtual ideas, how an actor thinks and how to be a good actress ...

Frederick, you're a con artist? I'm a real artist.

A scammer vs a scammer and hacker

Frederick complained very angrily, 'I should have trusted my gut feeling!!!!! Why did you send me this file????? This file is to track my physical location! We should compete on how much we love each other, not how much technology we have!!!!!!!!!!'

Frederick was proud that he was able to spot Selina's suspicious behaviour. After all, he had received a little bit of basic IT advice from his criminal group. But he was wrong. Selina had already captured his physical location (actual country) two months ago. She was trying to capture something much deeper than that.

Frederick sent her a screenshot to show her that her file did have a problem—a screenshot of alien codes.

Selina replied naughtily as if she was innocent, 'My love, what are you talking about? Why should I check your location? You're in New Zealand of course ... Hey, what do you think I'm doing? You think I'm a crazy engineer???'

Frederick still screamed angrily, 'How do you explain this other screenshot that shows your file has malware or spyware?'

Selina re-thought why Frederick showed her the screen of alien codes—he opened the executable file using notepad! Stupid! He thought that a computer virus was made up of germs and bacteria!!!! But … it gave Selina a hint on how to scam him further.

She replied to his alien code picture, 'Okay, tell me, what is that? What does that mean?'

She continued cheekily, 'Hahahaha, now I understand. You opened the file the wrong way. That's why it shows my file has a problem. Hahahaha!!! You are a well-educated man. How could you make such stupid mistake??? Hahaha … HAHAHAHAHAHAHAHA!'

Frederick, think about it! Selina is just a stupid victim. Victims are very honest. If she suspects you are fake, she would have already informed you, but she hasn't. She probably knows nothing. Selina is a real, professional engineer. She's not a scammer like you. I don't think she will scam you.

Now Frederick was confused. He was ashamed—he trusted he must have done something really stupid to make Selina laugh at him so much.

'Okay, we're not going to talk about it anymore.' He feared that if they continued on the topic, Selina would notice he was extraordinarily stupid, not at all a well-educated man.

Selina continued to laugh at him.

'Hey, I'm your husband-to-be. I deserve your respect!'

'Hahahahahaha, honey, I don't understand you. Why would someone want to know your actual location? And ... what's the problem if people know you are in New Zealand?'

Frederick said, 'Hey, you are a computer engineer, you should have checked your file before sending to me. You should be careful not to put me at risk.'

'Okay, it's my bad. So, I am not qualified to be your wife, right?'

'Honey, I always accept you as you are.' Frederick did not want Selina to leave due to his "mistake". 'We'll never talk about this incident again. After all, it was partially your fault for sending me the file and causing the confusion.'

He added, 'I am thinking of potentially bringing you to New Zealand to meet me soon.'

Frederick was definitely not in New Zealand. But if Selina did suspect he was lying, then she'd find out sooner or later. So, he decided to gamble: pretend as if he was really in New Zealand and ready to meet Selina there. Hopefully, by saying this, Selina would stop doubting.

< *Selina thought: I shouldn't challenge him too deeply. Otherwise, he'll suspect that I suspect he is fake. Then he'll refuse to do anything I want for fear that I'll use my tools to chase him. Let him relax for now.* >

A new romance scammer, Selina Co

To confuse Frederick further, Selina made up a lot of questions regarding their relationship. Selina said, 'My love, I want you to re-think our relationship. Look, maybe our characters are not suitable for a long-term relationship. These days, you never listen to what I say to you. I feel that talking to you is like talking to the air.'

'But I love you and you love me!' The young Frederick only knew the word "love" and knew nothing about lives.

'Love is not everything, we're talking about staying together for the rest of our lives. I'm calm and stable, while you're always panicking and rushing, and an awful listener. If our characters are so mismatched, it'll be painful for us to stay together, no matter how much we love each other.'

'No, we'll be happy together. I'll ensure it doesn't happen again. Now I've learnt I have to change for you.'

'Love you. 🖤'

Selina asked Frederick many rubbish questions—'Why do you love me so much?' 'How are we going to deal with our differences in characters and backgrounds?'—to make him believe that she was sincerely planning their future and still didn't know he was fake.

< *Selina thought: Frederick, spend more effort thinking of how to answer my questions, concentrate on me, invest more effort in convincing me how much you love me. Cos I need to hijack your mind—you're going to do whatever I want, when I find out how to capture your real identity.* >

Frederick's biggest weakness: GREED

Frederick hasn't received any money from Selina for a while.

He made a recording of himself crying, hoping it would touch Selina's heart.

Selina (pretended to) be sorry for him, 'Oh, my love, your tears! I've told you, I can't take your phone calls, cos I can't stand hearing you cry. Honey, you know, I miss you very much!' <*She thought: Frederick, why are you still online? Why haven't you been caught yet? When will I no longer need to entertain you?*>

Frederick cried, 'Honey, are you still going to help me out or not? If you aren't going to help me, please let me know, so that I know

I have no hope …' Obviously, he didn't want to spend more time on Selina if she wasn't going to give him more money. He'd rather concentrate on new victims.

Selina said, 'Honey, stop saying that. I can't afford to lose you. I've promised to help you, just like you have promised to pay me back my money.'

Frederick certainly didn't know what Selina implied. 'Love you, honey.'

Selina said, 'I'm doing everything I can for you.' These words were true. Selina was really doing everything possible for Frederick. She was setting up complex systems, programming, researching technical topics and solutions, researching news about romance scammers in Ghana, liaising with the polices, writing to the authorities and liaising with organisations from a few countries. And all in the hope of cracking Frederick. She hadn't worked this hard since she graduated from high school. (She was lazy in university.)

'Honey, don't let money separate us. I don't want to lose you,' said Frederick.

'My love, please get me out on bail. I'm going to die here.'

'My love, you won't die there. New Zealand custody is a safe place … Tell me the truth, what did the custody officers do to you? They didn't torture you, did they?'

'No, they didn't.'

'Honey, tell me. If they tortured you, I'll sue them!'

'No, they didn't torture me. It's just the environment here is terrible.'

'My love, you aren't in jail yet; you're only waiting to go to jail. It'll be worse when you're in jail. So, you're not doing too bad now.'

'How can you say this to me?'

'I want you to think positively. Life is a long journey and there are always harsh things to go through. So, let's face everything positively.'

Frederick didn't want to disagree or show their characters mismatched, otherwise, she may walk away.

'Yes, let's face it positively. Honey, I will wait for your bail. My love, don't let money separate us. I would rather die than lose you.'

In earlier days, Selina did make some effort thinking about how to scam Frederick. Later, she remembered Frederick probably had a few victims on hand at the same time and wouldn't remember the details of all dialogues. So she didn't need to pay a lot of attention to keeping her words very, very consistent.

Actor vs actress

To act well, there had to be two people inside this scammer "Frederick". One was the real him, a poor little nothing, living in a slum in Ghana. He was lazy and his full-time job was to find prey in Asian or Western countries on the Internet to scam. The other "Frederick" was the well-educated Frederick. He was a strong, independent civil engineer who loved his country the United States a lot. He was a good Christian and a kind man. He had money, a big house with four rooms, friends, social status, satisfactory work and a nice church life. But he had a lonely, hollow heart until he met his dream girl, Selina (or whatever the victim's name was when he was talking to them the other hours of the day).

Similarly, there were two Selinas. One was the real Selina A, who was dedicated to cracking this "Frederick". This Selina was liaising with different police forces and authorities, doing months of IT work and social studies, hoping to find a way to put Frederick in jail. The other Selina was Selina B, who desperately loved this

Frederick (as he wished). She was doing everything she could to save her husband-to-be Frederick Chong and was dedicated to building a lovely family with him ever after.

This Selina B still didn't know Frederick was fake. She analysed, she questioned and she expressed her deep love to this Frederick, trying to resolve Frederick's problems in a rational way.

Now Selina A had already captured a lot of information on this scammer Frederick, but it was still not sufficient. There was not enough time—she must keep him on line with her so that she can get his real identity and detailed geolocation. But she couldn't put Frederick on hold for long without satisfying his monetary requests. What should she do?

In fact, Selina was currently in Singapore for work. She didn't tell Frederick as she didn't want him to think she was tracing her funds there and had found he was fake.

Hang on, she can be in Singapore, why can't she be in another country?

Welcome to Selina's wonderland!

Selina B said, 'My love, the loan has arrived. I'll pay your agent tomorrow, so that you will be free. Once you get out of custody, will you fly to my home Australia immediately or will you stay in New Zealand for a while? Tomorrow evening, I'm flying to Palau for work for few days; I'll be back on Saturday. See you on Saturday 💟!'

'Congratulations to Selina 🧖🔟👸 and Frederick! I'm very grateful for all your help. You are my super woman! Have a good sleep. Talk tomorrow 💟,' Frederick said happily.

'Good night, my love 💟,' Selina B said with love and passion.

Eight months later …

'Honey, have you come back from Palau yet? I've been in custody for months now. The environment here is very harsh. Are you still getting me out or not?'

'My love, I have promised to get you out. Like you promised to give me back my money. I've told you I'm doing everything I can for you … Honey, your agent is behaving criminally. I've sent them the money to get you out on bail. How can they pretend they haven't received it?'

Frederick, do you trust the innocent victim Selina? Or do you trust your criminal syndicates? Frederick, go, have a fight with your criminal syndicate! It must be that Selina had already sent the money. Your criminal syndicates are pretending they've never received the money, so that they don't need to pay you. It's criminal behaviour. Go, have a fight with them!

Palau was once Selina's holiday destination—beautiful beaches, good for snorkelling, a land of coconuts. She was familiar with this place, so it was not difficult to make up a story that she was staying there for work.

Frederick said, 'If you don't get me out, they'll officially put me in jail, then I'll block you in Whatsapp and disappear from your life!' Frederick had lost his mind. Selina had been filling his head with dreams: you are getting USD 75,000 in a few days, you are getting USD 75,000 in a few days. Eight months had passed, and she was still saying, you are getting USD 75,000 in a few days.

Selina B felt hurt (while the real Selina A was sitting on her sofa, eating a carrot). 'Honey, how can you say this to me? I love you so much and have been doing everything for you … Now I wonder if you really love me or not … You actually plan to block me in Whatsapp and leave me once I help you pay the bail, don't you?'

Now, Frederick remembered he needed to suppress his angry feelings, 'No, I'd never do that to you. I love you very deeply, as the sun and the sky can witness! Honey, I don't want you to think negatively.'

'My love, we need to ensure we both are safe. After doing so many transfers for you, I'm in debt and you've lost all your money. I have to stay in Palau for work until my boss lets me come back to Australia so that we both can survive. How are you? I miss you very much …' said Selina B.

There was more dialogue. I am sure you can imagine that rubbish dialogue between an actor and an actress—well, it's not important, as long as you can find excuses.

Since then, the "couple" continue their love story: 'I love you, you love me.'

And Selina A gained the time to continue to analyse how to crack or catch this Frederick Chong, until she succeeds, or until she fails.

'My love,' Selina and Frederick vowed to each other, 'YOU ARE TOO IMPORTANT TO ME!!'

WHY TO SCAM/NOT SCAM YOUR SCAMMER

Some people feel proud or bold of telling scammers that they've found out they are fake. Actually, it is very wrong to do so. You are effectively giving feedback to scammers, teaching them what they did wrong and how they should improve their scams to harm more people. No wonder their scams have been improving so quickly! **You should not inform them that you know they are fake**. Instead, please let them continue to make the same mistake and continue to fail.

If you spot a scammer on the Internet, the first thing you should do is to report it to the dating website owner to block his/her profile. This helps save other people from being victimized. It also helps dating websites analyse patterns of Internet romance scammers and enhance their protection (if the website is ethical). You should also report it to your country's cybercrime squad, such as ACSC in Australia. This helps your government to get a better idea how many attacks there are and plan government resources and strategies accordingly.

The general advice is that you should immediately drop off the conversation and not to talk to the scammer anymore. One obvious reason is that many victims have been hoping the lies are true, especially those who have been under their spell for years. They may easily be convinced by the scammer's excuses and become re-victimized again. Another reason is that some victims have been blackmailed by scammers. Nevertheless, if you haven't sent them nude pictures, personal banking information, passport information or your address, they are not likely to have the real means to harm you. Finally, continuing to talk to the scammer does not reasonably help you track him down, unless you use IT tools to do so, or you've hired IT people to do so.

But, if you are certain you won't be trapped by the above situations, then I believe there is no harm in scamming your scammer. This way, you'll confuse them and make them spend more time and effort on you, so that he can scam fewer people.

There are scam-baiters doing this work, to kill scammers' time and effort, making them feel frustrated instead of excited and proud about scamming. It's not difficult to scam a scammer. Most of them are uneducated, uncivilized liars. If more people come out to confuse romance scammers, it would make their scamming difficult and unrewarding.

However, your own safety is the most important. Please consider the possible risks if you are going to do this.

My personal opinion is, it is good to scam a scammer; but if you are going to scam them, never let them know. It is not good to offend them too much.

COMPARISON: FREDERICK'S SCAM VS SELINA'S SCAM

	Frederick's scam against Selina	Selina's scam against Frederick
Nature	Romance scam (i.e., pretend to be in love)	Romance scam (i.e., pretend to be in love)
Scam Rubbish	*'I love you very much'*	*'I love you very much'*
Scam words	*'The sun and the sky know how much I love you.'*	*'I can't imagine losing you. I can't live without you.'*
Say what the victim wants to hear	√ Frederick said he was a good Christian, loved hockey, loved music, and had a Macau background. These matched Selina's hobbies and background according to her profile and probably what she wanted to hear.	√ Selina said she loved Frederick very deeply—this was what Frederick wanted to hear as it implied she would send all her money to save Frederick.
Make the victim dream	Frederick created a dream for Selina: 1. Married happily, with children 2. No need to work after marrying him 3. Permanent visa to the US	Selina created a dream for Frederick: 1. Sending out USD 75,000 in a few days
Timeline of promises	A few days later (you'll meet Frederick in person)	Tomorrow (Selina is going to send out USD 75,000)
Can the dream come true?	Never	Never
Offer repeated assurance that the dream will come true	Yes > 20 times	Yes > 15 times
Blackmail	Frederick blackmailed Selina, saying that if she didn't "lend" him money, his project would fail and she'd never meet or marry him. Later, he said that if she didn't "lend" him money for bail, then he'd be in jail and she'd lose him forever.	Selina blackmailed Frederick, saying that if he had a bad attitude towards her one more time, she'd let him stay in jail for the rest of his life (i.e., she wouldn't send the money).

Blackmail to break the perfect dream	√	√
Explicit blackmail?	Implicit	Implicit
Story nature	Virtual world	Virtual world on top of virtual world
Difficult level	Medium. Actors over the Internet don't have to worry about facial expressions or body language. But he was acting like a person with a very different character and background from himself (the real him was uneducated, with awful character; the character he acted was a successful engineer and a good Christian of great character).	Easy. Selina just acted like a version of the real Selina, except that the fake Selina didn't know that Frederick was fake. She sometimes created "incidences" to achieve her purposes or bring trouble to Frederick.
Isolation from friends and family	Scammers tend to isolate victims from their family and friends, as they may warn victims about scams.	Selina created stories to make Frederick distrust his criminal group and cause fights.
Intention	Get as much money from victims as possible, until victims' life savings are all used up and they've taken on their maximum debt to pay him.	1. Waste Frederick's time, effort and concentration, so that he can scam fewer people at the time. 2. Ruin his mind. Confuse his understanding of his virtual world and the virtual world on top of his virtual world. Make him unable to trust his victims, then the victims will not trust him in turn. 3. Create negative feelings in him. Make him feel frustrated and nervous about scamming. Make him feel that it's not a fun job. 4. Give him a perfect, beautiful dream of USD 75,000 coming in a few days, and break his dream. 5. Attempt to break his relationship with his criminal group. Make him believe the criminal group is deceiving him. He may end up offending his criminal group and being killed. 6. Wait for an opportunity to crack him. Put him in jail.
Say rubbish to confuse victim	√ E.g., Honey, it's not good to talk when you eat. Let's talk after your breakfast.	√ E.g., Love, I'm excited for this new year. I keep thinking of you. I know it'll be a year for you and me, I know we're going to meet soon!

HACKERS' MEETING

Hack or chat?

Hackers can be ethical or unethical. White hat hackers (ethical hackers) refer to good IT people who discover vulnerabilities in computer systems and report these to the organization to fix before bad, unethical hackers attack. Black hat hackers (unethical hackers) are those who find system vulnerabilities to attack for criminal purposes.

White hat hacking is a legal occupation. Some government departments or companies invite white hat hackers to discover system vulnerabilities and reward them if they're successful. But in general, if you are not invited to hack and you do it, then you can be caught and put in jail.

I'll soon be able to capture more information from the scammer, I'm only missing one small piece of code—I am pretty close!

There'll be a hackers' meeting tomorrow. Why not attend and see if anyone can give me some hints?

'Hi, I'm an IT consultant, Selina. Nice to meet you.'

'Hello, I'm Jeremy, a university student in environmental science. This is my girlfriend.'

'Oh, environment science is not that relevant to computers. Why would you two be interested in coming to this hackers' meeting?'

'Well, I love the way that people come together to discuss complex problems. I love the atmosphere of group study.'

I talked to those IT people, and I told them what had happened to me and why I wanted to get information from the scammer. Two hackers told me which websites I should go to that might possibly have the code I wanted.

I thought I'd got what I came for. I sat for another half hour, but nothing special was happening. I thought I should go home and continue my task.

'Selina, why don't you talk to Andy? He has a tricky mind.'

Why not? So, I went ahead and told Andy what had happened to me. I asked him if he had an idea on how I could obtain scammer Frederick's real identity or detailed geolocation.

Andy had a thought, and said, 'Let me have a cigarette. I'll be back.'

No hacking; go banking

Ten minutes later, Andy came back and took me to the backdoor of the venue. Sarah came with us as well.

'Selina.' Andy lit another cigarette. 'I think you should stop what you're trying to do. If you go one step further, you may potentially be accused of hacking. Then they may catch you, and close your case.'

'Really? I've read newspapers and government websites—they say my attempts are fine ... Okay, I'm not going to risk it. Let's put this project aside.' I physically closed my computer and put it to the side.

Andy continued, 'Also, even if you can legally get his identity and detailed geolocation, unless you can escalate it to the federal police, the state police will just say they don't have the power. Yeah, Sarah?'

Sarah nodded. 'Yes, the state police don't have the power to catch overseas criminals.' Pretty Sarah had been smiling sweetly the whole discussion, possibly because she had seen too many frauds as a hacker. And ... I like her.

I said, 'So, Andy, do you have any suggestions?'

Andy asked, 'Tell me, why did you send the money? What advantage did you get? How much money did you lose? And how did you send it?'

'It was a romance scam (embarrassed). I'd got no advantage by sending out my money. I lost 70% of my life savings, AUD 118,000.'

'S***!'

Suddenly, few partying gals and guys in the group came to the backdoor to smoke and chat. My discreet chat had become a big group discussion!

'Listen, the state police don't have the power to catch overseas scammers, only the federal police do. You, as an individual, cannot easily escalate your case to the federal police. But your bank can. Talk to your bank.'

'Okay.'

I told them more about my case.

'Hmm,' Andy said, 'Don't you notice? There's something wrong with your bank. Get yourself a lawyer.'

Jeff walked by. Andy asked him, 'Jeff, look, this is Selina's case. And it was what the bank did. What do you think?'

Jeff thought, and replied, 'How come??? It's very unusual.'

Andy asked Karen, 'Karen, this is Selina's case. What do you think?'

'That shouldn't have happened with banking transactions,' Karen replied.

'Selina, listen,' Andy turned back to me, 'It's not just me saying so, but also Jeff and Karen. Three people, all saying the same thing. We all think your bank has a problem.'

'Selina, talk to your bank. And get a lawyer. Also, go to the regulator.'

Who are hackers?

'Thank you, I will … By the way, I'm an IT consultant. What jobs do you guys do?'

Sarah said, 'I'm a data analyst. Jeff's a politician. Karen is an IT consultant. A few of us in this group work in banks.'

Andy said, 'I'm ex-federal police, specialized in investigating fraud. It's interesting, you come to this meeting to learn how to deal with your fraud case, and you happen to find a person who investigated fraud.'

I said, 'It's not a coincidence. Yesterday when I prayed and asked if I should come to this meeting, a voice told me I must come. So I had to come. I knew there must be something here.'

I said to Andy, 'Hey, that guy is dressed like a hacker!' *(photo I)*

That guy was Kenneth. He said (with no facial expression), 'No, I'm dressed like this because I'm cold … And there is no hacker outfit. Hackers are people that appear normal but do unusual things. And what's the original definition of a hacker? A hacker is defined as anyone who uses computer, networking or other skills to overcome technical problems. So, you and me, everyone here, everyone who does IT work, we're all classified as hackers.'

I originally thought this meeting was for both white hat hackers and black hat hackers. But now I knew, they were all good people. They were just curious, hard-working and nosy scientists who loved to learn tricky technologies. They were all white hat hackers!

As for me, I'm a … red hat! Because … a red hat is more beautiful (refer to the Alpaca company logo). I was wearing a long, red cloak—and I pulled up the hood so it resembled a typical hacker outfit.

* Refer to the last page of the book - Clarifications

Photo I: Symbolic "hacker outfit". Does it look like those dark-side people in Star Wars?

Photo J (suppressed): Frederick claimed he was holding his passport, preparing to go to the airport. (Refer to P. 85)

Selina felt that it didn't seem to be Frederick's hand. The bone structure and skin colour seemed very slightly different from the usual Frederick.

Photo K: (Refer to P. 85) Luggage for four months? And ... so old-fashioned! Not Frederick's style—he always wore high-quality suits.

Photo L: Can you tell the problem with this photo? Frederick said he was in business class.
(Refer to P. 86)

Photo M: Scammers can produce as many banking documents as they want. Who cares? They're in their own countries, and rarely get caught. (Refer to P. 86)

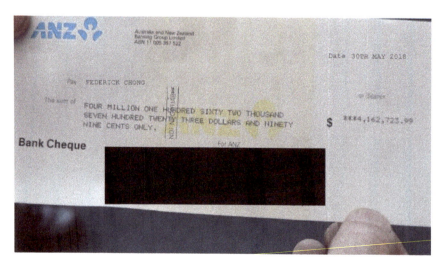

Problem with the image: 'the words are not parallel to each other,' said Inspector Haden. Furthermore, when Selina prepared this book, she noticed that the fonts of "Federick Chong" and the date are different from other contents.

Photo N: The top Baidu mythical Internet creature "Grass Mud Horse", created using the image of a real, innocent alpaca. (Refer to P. 185)

According to the Internet, the "Grass Mud Horse" is a lively, intelligent and tenacious animal. The background of the below picture is said to be the "Mahler Gobi Desert". You can find many music videos, cartoons and "documentaries" on the Internet about the "Grass Mud Horse", which describe in great detail its natural habitat, species, etc ...

In reality, the "Grass Mud Horse" does not actually exist. The "Grass Mud Horse" is only a vulgar play on words, having a very similar pronunciation as "f*** your mum" in Mandarin. The "Mahler Gobi Desert" and all documentaries on the "Grass Mud Horse" are fake. The background in the photo below is actually Bolivia.

Isn't that the same as Internet romance scams that faces get stolen to create virtual Internet profiles and fake stories?

As there is such a quantity of false information on the Internet, many adults are confused and call the real animal "Grass Mud Horse"! Some TV program producers and toy manufacturers have also become confused, and mistakenly label the real animal as "Grass Mud Horse"!

After all, it is what the Internet teaches them.

Now, you understand it is normal to get confused in Internet scams!!!!!

Photo O: Company logo of Selina's anti-romance scam company Alpaca Consulting IT Pty Ltd. (Refer to P. 186)

Selina moved the familiar alpaca faces to Bondi beach and dressed them up as IT detectives, using MS Windows tools only (without using Photoshop).

Do these obvious computer graphics make you think of how criminals create fake passports, fake banking documents and fake air tickets using computer graphics?

Same as romance scams: Do you believe an alpaca is talking to you because we put an alpaca picture into our profile?

LAWYERS

Justice?

Andy and Jeff suggested that I should talk to the banks first. 'Selina, remember to get some written proof that you have talked to the banks. Don't just discuss it with them verbally!'

I immediately discussed the case with my bank Hxxx in Australia and recipient bank Ixxx in Singapore. They both said they would look into the case, but soon I realized nothing was actually happening. Now, I had to get a lawyer.

Help? Or an another scam?

I called a number of lawyers in Australia specialized in banking, but when they heard the word S-C-A-M, almost all of them immediately said, 'Sorry, we don't deal with cases related to scams.'

Most phone calls were answered by solicitors or lawyers, and they said they didn't do scam cases. This one was answered by an officer in a law firm after I briefly explained my case. 'Okay. We do charge a fixed price of AUD 275 per half hour for you to speak to one of our lawyers. Do you want to talk to our lawyer?'

'So, what does that mean? What should I expect by paying the AUD 275? Am I going to talk to your lawyer, and then have them tell me they're not knowledgeable in this area?'

'Well … um … We do charge a fixed price of AUD 275 per half hour for our lawyer to listen to your case. But … I don't know what they can do for you …'

'So the AUD 275 is for hiring an audience to listen to my story? I pay AUD 275 to your lawyer to listen to my story, and there is no expectation about whether they even know this area or not?'

(Hesitation …) 'Our lawyer can listen to your case. But we do charge a fixed upfront fee of AUD 275 every half hour to talk to our lawyer …'

'You've told me three times that you want a fixed upfront fee. So, what should I expect by paying the fee? Can your lawyers help or not?'

(Frustration … Hesitation … A deep breath …) 'No.'

'Rubbish!' I hanged up.

Good lawyer

Eventually, one lawyer, David, called back.

'You can only sue a bank if it's done something wrong. For example, the bank processed things wrongly, or they facilitated an illegitimate bank account for criminals.'

He continued, 'As for scams, we've had a few clients who lost millions of dollars to scammers. They paid a lot of money to hire investigators, prepare all the evidence, and asked us to put it before the federal police. I don't know why, but the federal police are just not interested. At least, that was our experience.'

'Oh, okay …' I had a thought.

'For scam cases, law suits will cost victims huge amounts of money in an attempt to chase the thieves, but usually they don't get a cent back. By the way, how much did you lose?'

'AUD 118,000.'

'Woah, that's a lot of money! Why are so many people sending out a great deal of money to scammers, but when we trace solicitor fees, they are often late or unwilling to pay????? How did you lose the money?'

'Romance scam.' (embarrassed)

'Which Australian bank did you use?'

'Hxxx'

David said relaxingly, 'Why did you use this bank??? Hxxx is rubbish! It's famous for money laundering.'

I was surprised. 'How can that be possible? Hxxx is an international bank.'

'Watch a documentary called *"Dirty Money of Hxxx"*. It's on Foxtel.'

'Fox what again?' My poor English meant I didn't catch it.

David was still relaxing. 'F-O-X-T-E-L Foxtel. It has a documentary called *Dirty Money*, about Hxxx.'

'But I don't understand. I previously worked in banks. I understand that if a bank breaches the anti-money laundering laws in a country, the fine is very heavy.'

Now David became serious, 'They don't care. They just pay the fine. Many customers of Hxxx are criminals. They gain back the revenue from there.'

'Really??? But … They said they were doing a fraud investigation for me.'

'They say this to everyone. They're not really doing it.'

< *Then I had a thought: No wonder all the communication with Hxxx bank had only been on their own portal, instead of being via email. They wanted to make sure customers do not keep a copy of evidence that things had been brought to them. One Hxxx manager had emailed me about my case, leaving evidence. A few days later, the people in the branch looked at each other and said, 'She is no longer with the bank.' Perhaps she was fired for emailing me!* >

'Really! Ok … I'll check out the documentary. Thank you very much. By the way, I'm an IT consultant and I want to attempt to capture the scammer's real identity and detailed physical location using IT tools. Do you know at what point IT work is classified as legal and at what point it's classified as illegal? I'm not going to risk doing anything that might be illegal.'

'You need to talk to lawyer in this specific area. But the police have all the tools—you don't need to risk doing it yourself.'

'Thank you very much, David.'

He was very kind. Maybe he pitied me as I was a victim who had lost a fortune. Now, at least I knew I didn't need to do more IT work to chase the scammer.

Illegitimate bank account ... Hang on ... Hang on! That means I should chase from the Singapore side!

Bad lawyer

After short-listing, I selected a lawyer in Singapore, Neon. Neon was a Singaporean Chinese lawyer who had studied in the United States. His dual-background in both Singapore and a Western country should be beneficial to my case. He probably had a good understanding of Singaporean culture to deal with Western countries' affairs (Australia, in my case). Singapore society is Chinese dominated, and he is Chinese—an advantage. He was well-educated and had his own practice. He seemed very senior, and was quite handsome too! (Sorry, I have to mention that. You know, we artists are attentive to beautiful things. And being beautiful or handsome is good for impressions or presentation, somehow.)

After a short briefing about my case, Neon told me to email him more information. After that, he asked me for a solicitor fee of SGD 749, for a one-hour consultation and for examining the evidence.

He must have some ideas, otherwise, why would he ask me for SGD 700 (after bargaining) after asking me to send him details of my case?

An hour before the meeting, Neon sent me a totally irrelevant legal case to prove to me that he had done "some" studies, before going to a conference call. It had no similarities to my case, except that it was also against a bank.

This is how the conference call went. Neon started, 'So ... What do you want to sue the Chinese bank Ixxx for? You're making an assumption that banks shouldn't have illegitimate bank accounts. The only law you can use is tort. But as you are not their customer, the relationship to tort is weak.'

'This is not an assumption, Neon. I didn't have a chance to introduce myself—I was a banking consultant working in banks for years, including a bank in Singapore.'

'Your Western banks are stricter. Asian banks are not as strict in this area.'

'We're talking about regulatory requirements, not voluntary requirements.'

That meant Neon knew nothing but tort. Okay, he was a senior lawyer, but only specialized in tort.

He also attempted to explain romance scams to me. 'Some victims hire detectives to chase their scammers in African countries. You can guess how much they recover?'

'Zero.'

Astonished, he paused, then said, 'How do you know that?'

I thought it was public knowledge.

Neon continued to imply that he was knowledgeable. 'Most of the scammers that get caught in Nigeria are found to be bankrupt. I don't know why—possibly they give the money to family or girlfriends before going to jail.'

I said, 'Those idiot scammers are not educated and don't know to keep the money. Once they get the money, they immediately spend it on fancy cars and expensive hotels. When they have no money left, they sell those luxury items at very cheap prices, to buy food and toilet paper … if they use it. Also, some scammers are controlled by criminal groups, and the scammers themselves only get a portion. By the way, my scammer was in Ghana, not Nigeria. Those two African countries are very different.'

'You might need to face the fact that these scammers are very hard to chase. I also got scammed for a little bit of money, but I accepted I couldn't do much.'

That meant he had no solution. I asked, 'By the way, is it possible for me to go to the Singaporean regulator or the court myself without a lawyer?'

'That's a good question … Yes, but it'd be a waste of money, as they may need you to come to Singapore.'

< I thought: Paying him SGD 700 was an even greater waste of money. It was similar to the price of an air ticket from Australia to Singapore. >

Now, Neon wanted to tell me about IP addresses. 'It's very hard to chase scammers. They're good at faking things. They can fake their IP addresses.'

'I didn't have a chance to tell you that I'm an IT consultant. Just for your information … First, IP addresses cannot always be faked. Second, an IP address itself is not sufficient to learn a scammer's identity.'

He paused in surprise, and then asked, 'Not sufficient?????'

'No. An IP address is unique, but shared. For example, one thousand people share three IP addresses. Who is who?'

The meeting lasted for only 23 minutes, but he'd asked me to pay for a 60-minute consultation. Of course, Neon also didn't need to examine any evidence as included in the price, because he had no solution anyway. I felt that I had given him a consultation, rather than received one.

Actually, he might not be a very bad lawyer; he just wasn't knowledgeable in that area. At least, he agreed to refund back the SGD 700 to me. Now I understood why lawyers in Australia immediately shut their doors once they heard the word "SCAM"— Internet scams were relatively new. They weren't knowledgeable in this area and didn't want to take the risk.

No one can help? Then I'll help myself

Lawyers couldn't help my case. But there was a person who would certainly be willing to help without charge—the banking consultant (myself)!

Banks vs money laundering?

My plan with Chinese bank Ixxx in Singapore settled. What about my bank Hxxx?

Later, I met with Andy and the two other banking consultants again. We discussed my case against Hxxx bank.

'Lawyer David said your bank in Australia had done no wrong because you missed out the details. Your largest single transaction was AUD 49,600, which the bank was supposed to flag as suspicious, but they didn't,' said Andy.

He added, 'Think about it, just like when locals or foreigners travel to a country, you need to fill in a form, and you must declare big amounts of money or valuables over AUD 10,000 in customs.

Individuals can't just bring in or send out huge amounts of money whenever they like—they have to declare it. Under regulations in most developed countries, including Australia, in your case, your bank was supposed to have talked to you, checked with you on what had happened, whether it made economic sense, etc ... Because it can be money laundering or even a crime.'

'So ... You mean ... The transactions should not have gone through, even if I initialized them?'

Andy nodded.

'Another big problem is, a total of AUD 118,452.08 was sent out of Australia within 14 days by an individual. You are not a business owner, not a tycoon, Singapore is not even your hometown. It didn't make economic sense at all. It looked very likely to be either a crime or money laundering. Under anti-money laundering law in Australia, your bank Hxxx was supposed to flag this as suspicious and talk to both you and the regulator, and they didn't.'

Oh yes! Now I remembered what I had learnt when I worked at the banks: ongoing transaction monitoring, overseas transactions, customer due diligence! All staff and contractors at my bank were forced to take internal examinations in the first month of joining. This was to ensure we all fully understood the requirements on anti-money laundering and counter-terrorism financing laws. Every one of us had to get a high mark of at least 80 (or 90?) out of 100. Anyone not getting a high mark couldn't stay at the bank.

Yes, these transactions, according to anti-money laundering and counter-terrorism funding laws in most developed countries, must be flagged as suspicious. Failure to comply with anti-money laundering laws, such as failure to report suspicious transactions as per the guidelines, can send the bank staff involved to jail (which seems to rarely happen), or the bank will need to pay a very heavy fine (which often happens).

Based on what Lawyer David said, possibly Hxxx bank was intentionally negligent in the execution of ongoing transactions monitoring in overseas transactions. This would be for the convenience of their criminal customers, so they could launder money freely without warning and without letting regulators know!!! That was why my money had gone through! In other words, if my bank had followed Australian regulations, they should have flagged my transactions as suspicious from the second transaction (AUD 15,000), and talked to both myself and the regulator AUSTRAC about the likelihood of crime or money laundering.

According to the news, many victims stop their funds when their banks flag their transactions as suspicious and talk to them. According to the news, as an example, the *Commonwealth Bank* flags this type of transaction and talks to their customers, as Australian regulations require. Many victims end up deciding to stop the transfer, because they think, 'Even my bank says my transactions look suspicious. Maybe I'm really part of a crime?'

Sadly, I opened the bank account in Hxxx only a few months ago. If I'd kept all my money in my usual bank, *Commonwealth Bank*, instead of Hxxx, I would not have suffered such a huge loss!

Further, banks must report all cross-border transactions of AUD 10,000 or more to the regulator, AUSTRAC. This information is used to monitor money that might be going to crime gangs or terrorist networks. Mine were SGD 7,500, 15,000, 49,000, 3,000, 31,000 and 2,500—none were flagged by Hxxx nor Ixxx. (SGD was slightly higher than AUD on transaction dates.)

In my case, if Hxxx had followed Australian regulations and reported these transactions to AUSTRAC, Frederick's criminal group's illegitimate bank account in Singapore could have been investigated before I continued to send money! AUSTRAC might even have investigated me for sending these "interesting" funds. Then I would have been notified that I was being scammed and stopped sending further amounts.

Unfortunately, because of Hxxx's failure to follow Australian regulations, all this had not happened.

Based on what Lawyer David suggested, I researched news about bank failures in complying with anti-money laundering law. 'Oh my God! Both Hxxx and Ixxx are reported to have been terrible in complying with anti-money laundering laws internationally!'

(At the time of writing, it is not known whether or not Selina will be able to recover any of her money. Maybe 100%? Or maybe 0%. Further, please note that money recovery is affected by many factors, depending on your own case. The results of Selina's case do not necessarily apply to your case.

The purpose of this book is to tell people not even to risk paying a cent, because once you fall victim, it will be super hard to recover, while most cases are impossible.

Please also understand, we are IT experts, not legal consultants. The above discussion regarding legalities may be subject to inaccuracy.

One thing is for certain: in Selina's case, both Ixxx bank and Hxxx bank attempted to use the excuse 'You only logged the case with police, and forget to log it with us', to avoid having to pay compensation.

So, if you fall victim, remember to report the case to both police and ALL involved financial institutions.)

BANKS * WESTERN UNION * MONEYGRAM

Since the birth of Internet romance scams, Western Union and MoneyGram have frequently been manipulated by romance scammers. The scammers ask victims to make foreign transactions through without a trace, as recipients can remain anonymous.

Western Union and MoneyGram are relatively less regulated than banks. Nevertheless, it was said that Western Union compensated some scam victims who previously sent money to scammers through Western Union from the year 2004 to the start of year 2017. It was for a limited time only. I have not heard that anyone around me was compensated. Therefore, I am uncertain about the scale of compensation. Personally, I do not believe the compensation was massive—the news is still telling you money recovery in romance scams is usually zero, right?

In principle, sending money through banks is relatively safer than sending money through Western Union or MoneyGram. Having said that, if your banks have indeed not breached any laws in corresponding countries, then, to my understanding, they are still not liable.

Talking about countries, sending money to a least-developed country is much more dangerous than sending money to a developed country. Obviously, least-developed countries are still struggling to save their own people from hunger and to stop local crimes. They probably do not have the sufficient resources to care whether foreigners have lost money to their scammers. Also, governments of many of these countries can be corrupt.

Further, sending money within your country usually comes with more protections than sending money to a foreign developed country. First, if you are a citizen of the involved country, then reasonably, police have more responsibility to help you than a foreigner who does not even live there. Second, if the case only involves one country, then local police have access to everything. For example, they can access banking records and telco records without the need to escalate to your country's federal police and coordinate with other countries' federal police. This make things much easier.

Nevertheless, for any scam, you bear the biggest responsibility for protecting yourself from harm. You should reasonably check everything you can, instead of trusting your online lover blindly and expecting financial institutions to compensate you when you fall victim.

* *Alpaca Consulting IT Pty Ltd* was established to prevent people from falling victim and to stop existing victims paying even more. We are IT consultants, not legal consultants.

GHANA POLICE,
GHANA EMBASSY

And many government departments

Ghana

Four weeks after Selina found herself victimized, she had emailed Ghana police hq.pro@police.gov.gh about the event, with the IP address proving the attack was initialized by Ghana. Her email was ignored.

Perhaps they ignored it? Or perhaps the email address was wrong?

Five months later, Selina wrote another email to the Ghana police report.crime@police.gov.gh, with the IP address captured, the date and the time. This was also ignored.

She also attempted to contract the Ghana police through Twitter @GhPoliceService: And was again ignored.

After calling a few Australian government departments, they suggested she call the Ghana High Commission in Australia (in Canberra). Here was their reply:

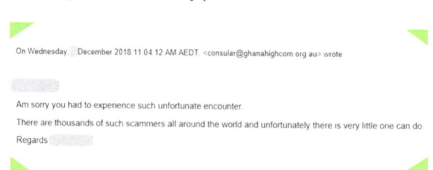

On Wednesday, December 2018 11 04 12 AM AEDT, <consular@ghanahighcom.org.au> wrote

Am sorry you had to experience such unfortunate encounter.
There are thousands of such scammers all around the world and unfortunately there is very little one can do.
Regards

Screenshot c: Email conversation with Ghana High Commission in Australia

Then Selina asked them for help to report the case to Ghana police; but they were unwilling to and asked her to report to Ghana police, who had always been ignoring her.

Writing to government departments

Ghana was unwilling to do anything to catch the scammers attacking Australia and APAC. What could Selina do? At the very least, she could write to Australian government departments, voicing her opinions on how to save other people from being victimized.

'I may not be able to save myself, but I hope I can save other people.'

Selina wrote to the Australian Competition and Consumer Commission (ACCC), hoping they would improve public education about the details of scams. In her opinion, her tragedy could have been avoided if she had been better informed of the **details** of scams.

She believed governments should provide details of scams to the **entire public** more proactively. They should not expect only those who are "fans" of scams to research and find their Scamwatch website.

She also pointed out that victims in the worst scams, "investment scams" and "romance scams", are usually **very well-educated, very successful people** in society. Yet they fall victim due to ignorance about scam details.

Selina also wrote to the Prime Minister's office, hoping the government could warn the public about the tricks and details of scams so that the public could protect themselves. It's also important to warn the public about possible fake passports and fake banking documents used by scammers.

The fact is, she was a typical victim, losing most of her life savings. There are many other victims. It is not infrequent to hear that some have lost their homes, which have been mortgaged for romance scams, while others have become bankrupt.

Selina also wrote to the Minister of Home Affairs, saying similar things.

Selina also wrote to the Communications Minister, hoping they would warn the public about the tricks and details of scams so that the public could protect themselves.

Selina wrote to Defence, suggesting the possibility that the AUD 24 million lost per year could have partially gone into the hands of terrorists or dangerous countries, funding their weapons.

Not only Australia, but countries like the US, the UK, Canada and Hong Kong are losing large amounts of money too. Most of this is not traced. Certain amounts could have gone into the hands of terrorists or dangerous countries, contributing to military forces for World War III.

Selina also wrote to the Foreign Minister, saying similar things.

Do what you can

Selina was only an individual, a little nothing. Her voice was weak. But as a citizen, she tried her best to express suggestions on how to avoid the same tragedy happening to other members of her country, and possibly other countries.

She could not say her opinions and suggestions were the most appropriate. The government surely had other things to consider and prioritize, but she tried her best to give suggestions to the best of her knowledge.

Campaign 1:

If you believe that United Nations and governments of countries currently under frequent attacks by Internet romance scammers should apply more pressure on Nigeria & Ghana to catch their Internet scammers and impose very heavy penalties towards those scammers, please "like" and share on Facebook:

https://www.facebook.com/selina.ko.5602/posts/109339826853661

Campaign 2:

If you think governments should educate the public more on the **DETAILS** of romance and investment scams, such as placing advertisements or documentary on the topic more frequently, please "**like**" and **share** on Facebook:

https://www.facebook.com/selina.ko.5602/posts/109342320186745/

SEARCH ENGINE OPTIMIZATION AND INCORPORATION

Professional romance scam IT detective—
prevention and victim services

In the Japanese language, 'alpaca' sounds like 'idiot'.

In China, an alpaca's face is used as a fake Internet animal (Grass Mud Horse) to represent people who are clever, naughty and say 'no' to threats.

In the real animal world, the sheep-like, ever-smiling alpacas are the natural enemies of wolves and foxes, kicking and killing them to protect sheep.

Difficult, but do not give up ... until you should

As Andy and lawyer David said, it was super difficult to get the federal police to investigate a romance scam case, even for individuals losing millions. But I was not going to give up.

What about gathering more people victimized by the same scammer or his criminal group? What about having 5 victims, 10 victims, or maybe 50 victims in the same case? Then I'd have a better chance! The police or myself could also get more information on the case from different victims, maybe enough to crack the case.

Okay, I am going to use my IT skills and experience in romance scams to help other victims identify romance scams. Then I can group victims of the same scammer or same scammer group together to make small individual cases become big cases. This will prove these cases are affecting Australian society much, and hopefully get some attention from the federal police.

Revolutionary IT evidence-based Internet scam detection

First, it is technically possible to do a background check on whether a website is legitimate or not. If a website is illegitimate, then the online lover who provided the website is also illegitimate.

Alternatively, it can also be quite easy to identify illegitimate email addresses (refer to Chapter 6), which proves the online lover to be fake.

Second, by capturing IP addresses of online lovers, you can often tell their actual geolocation. While online lovers claim they are in developed countries such as the United States or Europe, if they are scammers, their IP addresses will reveal their actual geolocation in a third world country such as Nigeria. Even if they try to fake their geolocation, the IP address analysis will still be a hint.

Third, scammers often support their stories using fake passports or fake banking documents. It is best to check with the authorities whether these are real or fake, but this may not be possible because of their privacy protection rules (refer to Chapter 4). Luckily, in many cases, fake passports or fake banking documents can be identified by examining the images of these documents.

Last but not least is to do a reverse photo check. However, not all reverse photo checks would result in hits. In other cases, reverse photo checks can give confusing results and would require further examination using background checks and my experience.

Not all types of the checking above always result in an outcome. For example, some fake online lovers claim they are US soldiers working in third world countries. In that case, examining their IP addresses (actual geolocation) would not prove anything. Luckily, because of the fact that Internet romance scammers are not hackers, they normally do not have sufficient skills to fake everything perfectly. Further, there are always technical limitations on the Internet. Even computer-savvy scammers cannot normally get through all technical checking by IT detectives.

Advertising my IT services: eBay

The easiest thing to do, without using my brain, was to put an advertisement on eBay and Gumtree. Gumtree was for more local work and the website expected the deal to happen face to face—this didn't suit my service, as I'm going to help the entire ANZ region.

eBay is good. It enables you to reach huge number of customers instantly. If you are selling goods, sometimes there are promotions, and you do not need to pay eBay for putting up an advertisement until your goods are sold. eBay charges you a percentage from the price at which you sold. But for me, as I'm selling services instead of goods, they always charge a fee to put up my advertising, something like $8.50 each piece? Now I have at least three services: i) capture of IP addresses, ii) photo identity check, and iii) victim database. That means I need to pay $25.50 to eBay, whether there is a customer or not. But the bigger problem is that my service requires a lot of interaction with customers—getting more information about the online lover, clarification, photos, details of the layout, whether they had phone calls or real-life video calls, etc. While eBay does allow you to upload photos or attachments in the conversation, it doesn't allow sellers to directly contact customers without going through them, nor exchange of phone numbers or emails. So this customer communication channel is a bit messy. Many people, myself and my customers included, have never sent messages or attach files for a seller through eBay, so this will be a barrier.

Another major problem is that putting my services here … It just doesn't look professional. How can a professional IT service advertise services on eBay and not even have its own website? That's not right. I consider my work very professional. I should try to build my own website.

Professional website

I came across *hostpapa.com* (I think a few other website hosts are also good). It is quite cheap and includes a website builder for creating a website easily. In about four days, I had built a professional, beautiful-looking website with three tabs. And the technical support isn't bad—they're able to resolve problems and give suggestions on things that I didn't know as a newbie.

I actually needed four tabs. But the very cheap plan I use only includes three. If I want more, I need to upgrade and pay about $10 more monthly. And this is a MONTHLY fee, not a one-off. As an IT consultant, I attempted to get through by creating the extra page by doing my own coding.

The coding needs to be written in .php, which I was totally unfamiliar with. If it were in html, it would be straightforward. But with .php, I needed to do some study. I borrowed a book from the library but it wasn't very useful in my situation. So, I researched on the Internet on tutorials and basic concepts, made some attempts, and built two extra tabs using my own .php code—not very difficult.

I terminated my ad in eBay and moved everything to my own company website.

Too many victims

Then came another challenge: My website couldn't be found in a Google or a Yahoo search! This makes it useless! I built a website as I want the public to be able to see it by only searching Google or Yahoo. I don't want to pay a fortune for advertising all the time.

After discussing with hostpapa technical support, they said I should do some search engine optimization (SEO). So, I looked for documents and forums about the rules and how to make my website more searchable on Google and Bing.

SEO is a marketing discipline focusing on growing visibility in non-paid search engine results, making a page come up more frequently with a higher rank in the search results for search engines such as Google or Bing.

Google has disclosed how a Google search works:

Crawling – to make sure Google knows what pages exist on the web.

Indexing – for Google to understand what the pages are about.

Serving and ranking – so Google can determine the highest-quality answers and factor in other considerations that provide the best user experience and most appropriate answer when people search in Google.

You will find the best information on how Google SEO works by looking into their websites.

I created a sitemap, added internal links, added my company information in business directories, created LinkedIn and Twitter profiles to increase external links pointing towards my website, created a sub-menu and added metadata. These made my website look well organized and reliable, and are favourable for SEO purposes.

Further, a Google search favours informative websites. For example, if your website is about dogs, adding hundreds or thousands of mentions of the word "dog" will not pull your website to the top of the list in a Google search. Instead, if your website provides information on different aspects, such as dog breeds, dog care, why dogs are adorable, functions of dogs, health concerns, costs and cautions, then it is considered a comprehensive analysis and favourable for SEO.

Therefore, I decided to make my website informative—include analysis of all aspects of romance scams, make it as comprehensive as possible. I gathered news, victim stories, analysis, government announcements, statistics, reports from government websites, news websites, university analysis, romance scam campaigns, romance scam baiters and financial companies all around the world.

> *Perth: A widow lost AUD 600,000, went bankrupt and lost her job and her car.*

> *Hong Kong: A business woman lost USD 23 million.*

Official numbers: In 2018 alone, Australians lost AUD 24.6 million, with 3,981 reports and 30.8% experiencing monetary losses (plus an estimated 70–90% cases unreported due to embarrassment).

London: A woman lost her life savings. After that, she was conned into money laundering for her scammer, helping him to steal money from other victims.

United States: Victims are turned into money mules for money laundering—conduits for funds stolen from corporations and other victims.

Sydney: A grandmother sentenced to death by a Malaysian court for drug trafficking—she carried a bag for a fake online lover, which was found to be full of drugs.

England: British professor Paul Frampton was arrested in 2012 at Buenos Aires Airport with 2 kg of cocaine, and sentenced to four years and eight months in prison. The renowned physicist believed he was taking a suitcase to a voluptuous 32-year-old brunette he had fallen for online.

Australia: Disability pensioner John Warwick died in a Chinese police hospital in 2015 awaiting trial for drug trafficking.

Red flags = guess = no evidence

There are too many cases, too many victims! That's enough! According to the news, when victims pay money, most of them doubt whether their Internet lovers are real or fake. But they can't find a reliable answer. Potential victims are relying on "signs" or "red flags" that it may be a scam. Does that mean the best they can do is to guess? If they are lucky, they may find their fake lover's photo on the Internet to confirm a scam. Otherwise, there is no reliable way, forcing them to gamble between losing a true love and losing money!

In the case that the Internet lover turns out to be real, if they stop paying money now, they'll lose a significant person in their life. Many do not dare risking it and decide to pay. Once they start paying, they don't dare to stop, or they would have to immediately accuse themselves of having sent money for being scammed, and acknowledging money already paid will certainly go for nothing. So, many continue to pay, pay more and more, hoping the lover turns out to be real. This is how many victims end up losing their life savings.

Criminals enhancing their skills faster than governments

Unfortunately, criminals have been enhancing their skills quickly. For example, in 2018, the *Little Black Book of Scams* published by the Australian government was still telling the public that online lovers would refuse real-time video calls if they are scammers. However, in the same year, I had already spotted a few Internet romance scammers faking low-quality real-time video calls by playing recorded videos.

Governments have also told the public to identify Internet romance scammers by doing reverse photo checks; however, many scammers are now using photos that are not searchable using reverse photo checks.

Enthusiastic criminals

Since my website and my book were released, records show people in third world countries trying to study my book and my website. In contrast, people in developed countries are not as enthusiastic—everyone just believes the crime can't possibly happen to himself/herself.

Helpless victims and potential victims

Due to the high volume of victims and complexity of Internet scams, some victims who later report their cases to the police or cybercrime squad never know whether they were actually scammed or they'd encountered their true love, who disappeared from the Internet because of an accident or another unknown reason. A few end up hiring professional hackers just to get an answer.

For other individuals who have confirmed they are victims, most never even know which country initiated the attack. They only know what the police have told them, that 'it's likely to be Nigeria'. But romance scammers can also be from other African countries, Malaysia, the Philippines or other countries.

From the impact point of view, although victims can be any age, some victims who lose their life savings are close to retirement age—they can never gain that money back! I am young, even if I cannot recover my money, I can work hard to gain it back; but older victims are losing everything! This needs to stop!

I have spent months investigating how to identify romance scammers using reliable IT evidence. Why shouldn't I use my skills to help the public?

Then I recall the morning that I was running all around to seek help, looking for someone who could have given me a definite answer whether the Frederick had been real or fake. But no one could help …

'I won't let it happen to other people!'

I decided to take two to three months off work to concentrate on the fight against romance scams. 'If I can save two to three people from losing their life savings to romance scams, then it's worth it. Maybe I can save 20 to 30 people? What about hundreds?'

Remove misunderstandings and identify outdated tricks

I gathered information from news, victim stories, university analysis, government announcements, statistics, psychologists, socialists, general analysis, romance scam campaigners and baiters' websites all around the world. I found that many have certain misunderstandings, incompleteness or outdated information.

> 'No, not all romance scammers rely on pre-written scripts. Some scammers do have a good command of English, because English is an official language in both Ghana and Nigeria.'

> 'No, romance scammers are not clever, dangerous, nor high-tech people. They are only full-time liars.'

> 'No, some victims pay their life savings not mainly because of love, but because they've already paid some money and cannot accept the fact that they've paid a lot for nothing, so they continue to "gamble".'

I gathered information from newspapers and government websites internationally. Then I summarized new and old scammers' techniques and tricks to cover all known cases. I used my IT technical findings to identify criminals' limitations, removed misunderstandings from the Internet and rebuilt a more comprehensive analysis that covered all aspects of romance scams that I could think of. I highlighted a few cases as references for readers' ease of understanding.

'My website needs to be comprehensive. It needs to provide information to the public on every aspect of romance scams. However, criminal romance scammers may also read my website. My website must not disclose analysis that would help criminals improve their scams.'

'Each piece of analysis that I display needs to be as accurate as possible. If it is not accurate, I would rather not write it. For those that I write, I need to think about the limitations—for example, my analysis needs to be accurate to the best of my knowledge and as of the day of writing. Criminals can always innovate to enhance their scams; however, there are technical limitations that they can never change.'

It took me about two months to prepare a comprehensive analysis of romance scams and put this on my website. This took even longer than the technical work that I did to capture Frederick's IP addresses and machine information. I wanted to make my findings high quality and as complete as possible.

The unusual Selina

Now I understand: because most victims classify themselves as being "in love" with the fake lover, they blame themselves for wrongly falling "in love" and diminish other causes. As for me, I didn't actually fall in love with Frederick. I fell into the trap because of my wish to have a family, and because of his fake US passport and fake banking documents. Others probably fall victim because of hollow promises, such as "no need to work after we get married" or "guaranteed migration visa to the US". This is not LOVE, but hollow promises of a beautiful future.

Also, because IT experts rarely fall victim to Internet romance scams, most IT experts do not understand victim psychology. Therefore, they are probably not as dedicated to studying detailed romance scam layouts; those who are dedicated to studying detailed romance scam layouts and understand victim psychology do not understand IT very well.

Now, I'm an expert on both sides. I'm the natural enemy of romance scams!

Advertising and marketing

I had already done all the SEO I could, and received a SEO score of 95 out of 100, according to certain analysis. Yet Google still rarely showed my website in search results, so the public wouldn't know about my website.

One possible reason might be that the term "romance scam" was relatively new and not a hot topic. Google search logic might not have much development in this search term. Another likely reason was that there were not many external links referring to my website—this was unfavourable for SEO performance. Finally, Google search tended to output more popular websites, but my website was too new and not yet known by many at that time.

I decided to put an advertisement in Google search. In Google search, some keywords are more expensive, some are cheaper. Luckily, my website was about online dating fraud or romance scams, which attracted very few advertisements. Therefore, the advertisement price per click was relatively cheap.

I also put my story into this book to increase public awareness and understanding of the problem of romance scams. 'I need to make this book high quality, realistic, fun and informative. Everyone is my target audience, because no one believes they are going to fall victim—until it happens.'

Incorporation

Here came another challenge: for some reason, I needed to incorporate a company, instead of just a getting a business name.

While many people dream of running their own companies, I was a laid back person. I only wanted to be an employee with a stable income. I didn't want to build my own company.

But in the long run, there are advantages in doing so. For example, it might be easier to reach organizations or governmental bodies by having a company rather than appearing as an individual.

After a few days' thought, I decided to go ahead and incorporate a company. What would be the name of the company? Without a thought, the word "Alpaca" came to my mind, because I love alpacas. So, I just called it "Alpaca Consulting", as it's an IT consulting company.

As the name "Alpaca Consulting" was in use by an America company, I couldn't use it. So, I took the name "Alpaca Consulting IT Pty Ltd".

The alpaca

One day, I went to a business event. A guy asked, 'Why did you call your business "alpaca", not "tiger"? It's just a stupid sheep!'

I said, 'Well, coz the alpaca is a strong guard animal which protects sheep by kicking and killing wolves and foxes.'

Everyone was silent for a few seconds. Then he said, 'Just tell the truth—you just love that animal!'

Okay, my excuse was not convincing enough, so let me re-think … Why do I love alpacas in the first place?

Because it's a confusing animal—this sheep-like, ever-smiling creature is actually an excellent guard animal for sheep, kicking and killing wolves and foxes.

The alpaca is a camelid with no hump. It is a real animal, but is virtual to almost all of the world, as most people can only see it on the Internet. The alpaca's face is even used in certain countries as the **top mythical Internet creature**, the "Grass Mud Horse". *(Photo N)*

The alpaca's nature is as confusing as romance scams. Many adults in different parts of the world are still arguing about whether the alpaca is a real animal or a virtual image created with computer graphics! And even for those who know alpacas are real, many have confused it with "sheep", "llamas" and the fake animal "Grass Mud Horses".

Look at the sheep-like, fluffy alpaca, how can you expect it can kill wolves and foxes? Look at Selina's naive and lovely face, how can you expect she is a dangerous threat towards romance scams criminals?

Let the alpaca be the natural enemy against Internet romance scams! *(Photo O)*

Connecting with other campaigners

I reached out to certain known romance scam campaigners in the ANZ region to strengthen the forces in the fight against romance scams. I contacted Sharon Armstrong, who was imprisoned for more than two years when she was conned into drug trafficking by a romance scammer. She is now a dedicated campaigner protecting other people from being victimized and helping victims in various aspects. She is a well-educated, careful, clever and good-hearted woman. I also attempted to approach Jane Marshell, a famous romance scam speaker and writer in Australia, who lost $260,000.

In the future, I also plan to liaise with other romance scam campaigners or baiters around the world, to contribute to strong and robust strategies in the international game against romance scams.

Pricing

IT work is labour intensive. As I am not receiving donations from the public nor receiving government funding as of time of writing, our work must incur a fee.

My work is on romance scam prevention, to secure money and possibly the safety of individuals. To protect their own money, it is reasonable for them to pay, rather than making taxpayers or myself to cover all costs. As I am only charging a hundred dollars or so, it is affordable, too affordable.

We don't need to be free-of-charge to do a good deed.

'For labourer is worthy of his hire.' Luke 10:7

Another obvious reason to charge this small fee is to avoid abuse of our services. **With my limited resources, I want to save the maximum number of people from falling victim.** In many cases, members of the public should be able to identify romance scams by reading the romance scam analysis on my company website. But in more complex cases, they may need my help. By incurring a fee for my services, those who can DIY can resolve the problem themselves, and I'll help those who genuinely need me.

However, I'm not going to charge a high price for our services. If the price is too high, it discourages the public from checking their online lover's identity. I would rather set a low price to encourage them to check, so that fewer people fall victim.

Further, my aim in setting up this company is to root out romance scams. I am not intending with making my work sustainable or highly profitable. Instead, I will celebrate on the day that Internet romance scams are completely rooted out and no one needs my services any more.

Finally, the price I set is too low for professional IT work. I will need full-time IT work to survive; Alpaca will only be my part-time business.

'I would rather the public read my website to understand romance scams, so that they can protect themselves without my IT services; but I would rather they request my IT services than fall victim.'

Money gained from my services will also contribute to advertisement fees, so that more people see the detailed romance scam analysis on my website, and are thus saved from harm.

Lovers with "many small things" unusual

Many people do not want to pay a cent to check their Internet lovers. In these cases, my suggestion to them is that if their lovers have "many small things" that are weird, they should consider their lovers as fake.

Scoping

As we are receiving little money, I need to have my own full-time commercial IT work (as in the past) to survive. Therefore, Alpaca will only have limited resources. Our scope of work includes a) helping the public to confirm romance scams so that they do not fall victim, b) helping existing victims identify romance scam so they can stop paying their fake online lovers, and c) helping existing victims to get an answer on which countries the scammers are located in. The police will decide if they are going to trace the scammers further or not. Identifying actual attacking countries will also help the government understand which countries are attacking us and to what degree. They can then decide their strategies and policies to fight against the problem.

'We are not going to help victims recover money. My purpose is to tell them not to risk paying their online lover because it's highly unlikely they'll be able to recover a single cent after falling victim, as of the time of writing.'

'I would rather help more people avoid falling victim than spend a great deal of effort helping a few individuals recover their money, which is rarely successful.'

'Recovering money is a much more difficult task and is bound by regulations of the countries involved and how you actually lost the money. If victims still want to attempt this, they can choose to hire professional cybercrime investigators and lawyers. However, this would probably be much more expensive. According to lawyers, newspapers and my own experience, the money paid to chase the funds is not proportional to how much you can recover …'

'If someone is struggling about whether to pay his/her online lover, they need to know if they decide to pay, they shouldn't expect a single cent to be recovered ...'

So, let me focus on prevention work!

Real-life romance scams

As a professional service, I carefully considered the scope of my work on romance scams.

After careful consideration, real-life romance scams were found to have different layouts. In addition to the real-life romance scams in Chapter 2, here are some other examples of real-life romance scams according to TV documentaries:

- *A teenage girl knew a brilliant boy on the Internet who lived in another state in Australia. After about two years' dialogue, the boy said his father would come to deliver a small gift and stay at her home for few days. But while he was staying at their home, the girl's mother noticed something wrong with the man and expelled him.*

  Later, the boy asked the girl for a date and told her not to inform her mother. The girl went, and never came back. In fact, the boy had never existed. It had always been the fake "father" who pretended to be the boy and had been talking to her for the two years. She was raped and murdered.

- *A woman was newly married to a man she met on the Internet. One day, she saw his identification card in his wallet and found that his real name was not what he claimed it to be. She then searched for his photo on the Internet and found that this man had been "married" several times to different women and he already had seven children.*

  By that time, that woman was also pregnant, but she decided to abort and end the nightmare.

- *A woman was happily married to a rich, successful lawyer. The rich lawyer, who loved her very much, suggested buying a castle, which they did, and paid a lot to renovate. Later, she found that he had actually never been a lawyer; he'd only hoped to be. He lied to himself and the world. Finally, he left her, leaving behind a big bill for the renovation of the castle and lots of credit card bills.*

Real-life romance scams are too broad. The skills required are also different. I decided to define myself as an expert in Internet romance scam attacks by overseas scammers. This would be good enough to help many people.

As for local real-life romance scams, people need to use real-life approaches to identify scams, such as checking IDs and criminal records, talking to their family and friends, and being smart and vigilant.

Not-for-profit or profitable?

In principle, *Alpaca Consulting IT Pty Ltd* was established for the purpose of stopping people being victimized by romance scams. Our pricing is too low for IT work. We can barely make a profit. I think we are qualified to register as a not-for-profit.

However, if we register as a not-for profit, there are more regulations to follow and we would probably need to hire admin people just to manage the requirements.

I want to do more real work to help people, not a whole bunch of admin tasks. We don't need to be an NGO to do a good deed.

Thus, the company was registered as profitable, but the profit made by the entire company is expected to be less than the salary of a director in a typical charitable organization …

More scam-related IT studies

'If I'm going to provide services to the public, I need to ensure my work is professional.'

I tested out how to create fake Whatsapp phone numbers as criminals often do. (Remember Frederick was using a US phone number for Whatsapp?) I also further studied Internet scam-related topics such as technical flexibility and limitation of caller ID spoofing, fake websites and IP addresses.

'It is a pursuit of excellence.'

Originally, I offered to provide IT services to the public because I wanted to gather more victims related to my case, with the hope to escalate my case to the federal police. But it turned out that my case had already been escalated before I started providing my IT services to the public …

Thus, in the end, my website is only for helping other people.

WHAT'S THE CATCH?

Cats or mice?

It was how it happened:

Half a year after Selina reported her case to the Australian police …

As usual, I created rubbish topics to confuse Frederick. One day, I unintentionally made him nervous, and he rushed in talking to me. When he was nervous, he could easily make mistakes. Or, if not mistakes, he gave me hints I could combat him with.

I said, 'Love, I'm disappointed with you.'

Frederick asked, 'Honey, what happened? Why are you disappointed?'

But I was offline. Frederick rushed to comfort me by all means, so he re-created his profile on Meetup.com. (His original profile was blocked some time after I reported my case to the police— someone else reported his mis-behaviour to Meetup.com at that time.)

Resurrection

Now, a sudden Meetup.com message from Frederick popped up on my phone, 'Honey, I'm here.'

I was shocked! How could a person who was banned re-join whenever he liked??

I went to my personal computer to login to Meetup.com, hoping to report the security concerns. Once I opened the website, I found myself automatically logged in to my old Meetup account in Macau. I'd had a separated Meetup account as a Meetup organizer in Macau. An event invitation immediately popped up—an organizer meeting in Sydney on the coming Thursday. I was invited.

There was one spot left. I immediately took it. 'I'm going to discuss this with their management team in person.'

In the meeting, everyone did the usual socializing. I reached out to a representative, Colin, from the Meetup.com organization. I explained how I was approached by a scammer there, losing AUD 118,000, and that I'd captured information on the scammer but he remained at large.

'Colin, I hope you and Meetup.com report this case to the police. I'm only an individual, I don't have the power to escalate my case to Interpol. But Meetup.com is a huge organization serving thousands or millions of people around the world. If Meetup.com reports the case to the police, they'd probably escalate it. I suggest you report it to the FBI as well, because you're a US organization, or you can just report it to the Australian police, so that they can escalate my case, hopefully.'

The threats

I gave some news urls to Colin to show him how serious the problem of romance scams currently was. People in Australia, the UK, Hong Kong, the US and Canada, among others, were becoming bankrupt for romance scams. Some victims were used as mules for drug trafficking for their Internet "lovers", putting them in foreign jails. Lucky ones, like myself, only lost 70% of their life savings; others were forced to sell their homes to pay off the debt they'd incurred from the scam. Some lost their jobs.

I also showed him external findings on geolocation analysis of romance scammers and suggested Meetup.com consider certain technological solutions in preventing this crime.

Colin said, 'I'll convey your messages to the US headquarters of Meetup.com in New York.'

Escalated, eventually ...

Colin also attempted to help me report my case to the police to escalate it. However, only later did I realize that my case was actually already with Interpol. Possibly this was because I'd told the police that I'd like to attempt to recover my money from a developed country, Singapore, where my money was sent and had disappeared, instead of chasing Ghana, considered the second-largest centre for Internet romance scammers.

It might also be due to all the IT work I had done to analyse the case, giving solid hints about the actual layout of the crime. It may also be because of the fake passport and banking documents, which made it a much more serious crime. (Most romance scams are "love based" or "confidence fraud", but my case was "fake passport and fake banking document based"). Or, it may be due to the fact that this criminal group had multiple bank accounts in developed countries, including Australia and Singapore. This implied they have syndicates in our countries. I am not certain why, but surely, it was escalated.

Inspector Haden called me, 'Lady, your case is now with Singapore Interpol. They have a few questions for you. First, when did you last have contact with the scammer Frederick?'

'I didn't want to lose him, so I've made him believe I was going to send him more money. I've kept him online with me until now.'

My hard work paid off.

Criminal's bank accounts in our countries

'Inspector Haden, I have a question for you. How did they open bank accounts in both Australia and Singapore? Even if they have a bank account there, how can they possibly launder the money untraced out of our countries?'

Haden said, 'We don't know. The Australian bank account owned by Frederick's criminal group has had no movement. We haven't traced it down further.'

Okay. Now, as criminals have stolen my money from Singapore, when Singapore Interpol and Singapore banking regulator look into my case, they should be able to tell how my money had been taken.

I believe there are few possibilities:

i) According to the news, some victims are used as mules to help criminals launder other victims' money from developed countries to other countries. Because many other victims like me are only comfortable sending money within developed countries, criminals ask them to send money to their money mule. Money mules are also victims of romance scams. They help to forward the money to Nigeria or Ghana, for example.

Why would money mule help these criminals? Simple—they're also romance scam victims, they've usually have already lost most of their life savings. As explained earlier, when they have already lost a lot of money in a romance scam, they naturally lose their mind and can no longer question their scammers. How could they accept the fact that they've already lost everything for a big lie? So they simply don't doubt the scammers anymore and do whatever they tell them to—launder money, carry bags (which turn out to contain drugs) …

ii) Some (possibly not the majority of) romance scams are international criminal groups, controlled by senior members in developed countries. In today's globalised world, the same as legitimate companies, they take advantage of different countries and hire offshore human resources.

Romance scam international criminal groups take advantage of low prosecution rates and light penalties in third-world countries, such as Nigeria and Ghana. They hire offshore actors and actresses to be romance scammers. Meanwhile, senior members in developed countries do the management or possibly IT tasks at the back end, and gain most of the dirty money, leaving only a small portion for their African actors and actresses. Crimes run by these international groups could be relatively well-organized.

iii) The entire criminal group is in Ghana and/or Nigeria, but they somehow have a way to open bank accounts in Singapore and Australia remotely, and send out the money electrically without a trace—this is not likely. If this could be done easily, all African criminal groups would have done this.

For Frederick's criminal group, they had at least three different bank accounts in Singapore and one in Australia, involving three different bank account owner names. It is not likely to be case i) as there shouldn't be so many money mules; I guess it is likely to be case ii) (they have syndicates in Australia and Singapore)!

We will know the answer when Singapore gives us an update.

On behalf of the real Frederick

A day before Haden informed me that my case had already been with Interpol for a while, I had also submitted the case to the FBI through https://complaint.ic3.gov on behalf of Franco Yeung, whose face was stolen by scammer Frederick. I'd seen this FBI website in two pieces of news. Given my case involved fake US passports and fake US JP Morgan Chase banking documents, and the fact that the US government officer Franco had had his photos stolen to create scammer profiles, I believed it was appropriate to report it to the FBI. Let the FBI decide whether they wanted to look at it or not.

According to certain news, apparently, even if you are not related to the US, you may still report your Internet crime case to the FBI through that website. This helps the FBI learn how much impact a particular criminal group has had internationally. This also enhances the understanding on that particular romance scam criminal group, as it may be related to other existing cases. And you may even report on behalf of another person, like I did.

Boundaries

'Selina, about your company fighting against romance scams, don't you worry that you will be offending too many criminals and they'll want to kill you? They've been gaining a fortune from romance scams!'

Yes, Alpaca Consulting IT is not going to take over all cases from all countries in the world. Otherwise, I'd be killing the income stream for these criminals and they'd do everything they could to kill me. I will only oversee the ANZ area, and possibly assist Hong Kong and Japan who have only recently been attacked by this crime and therefore are relatively vulnerable. If other governments want me to help, I'll give advice—but they have to decide.

> *Ecclesiastes 7:16-17 'Do not be overly righteous, nor be overly wise; Why should you destroy yourself?*
>
> *'Do not be overly wicked, nor be foolish; Why should you die before your time?'*

Yes, Frederick Chong, from the day you knew I was an IT consultant, you should have walked away immediately. You should have thought about your boundaries. If you had not scammed a strong IT consultant and stolen so much money from her, you would have been able to live longer. I don't know whether Interpol will successfully catch you or not. Even if not, you have created a strong romance scam IT detective and campaigner, vastly destroying incomes of criminal groups that you belong to and all similar ones. You'd better wish you stay in jail, or you'll soon be killed by criminals of your kind in revenge.

This is the end of a book, but the start of a long campaign.

Selina sat down by Sydney harbour, as usual. She looked at the beautiful harbour, looked at the stars and the moon, and thought, 'Jason, why are you so important to me?'

As of the time of writing ...

Frederick Chong

... no longer stays online till 4 am Ghana time. Probably he's no longer scamming many victims by pretending to be a handsome man in New York. It is believed that he is over-obsessed with the dream of Selina's USD 75,000, and can no longer concentrate on new victims, who usually start with only a few thousand dollars.

There are also signs that he has suffered a certain level of emotional strain after Selina's year-long psychological torture—the same torture he had been doling out to his own victims.

Selina is still hoping to see him in jail one day. Selina has captured nine additional IP addresses and a few more illegitimate bank accounts in New Zealand, Australia, Malaysia and the United States.

In early 2019, Frederick changed his fake Whatsapp US phone number, possibly to avoid a police trace; but as he believed Selina was going to pay him more money, he informed Selina about his new, fake Whatsapp US phone number. Selina immediately informed the police.

Selina is amazed that Frederick the scammer has still not realized that he has been scammed by her for 1.5 years. Selina continues to keep him online without losing him.

Hxxx bank

... claimed to have started a fraud investigation for Selina. After Selina's frequent pushing, Hxxx finally requested Ixxx bank to recall the funds 1.5 months later.

3.5 months after Hxxx claimed to have started the fraud investigation, Hxxx said that they don't actually provide a fraud report for romance scams.

The case was brought to regulator F. Hxxx explained to regulator F that because they are busy, they do not have the time to check with customers whether overseas transactions are suspicious. < i.e. they do not really care whether customers are criminals laundering money or funding terrorists, or whether customers' account can be hacked, or whether customers have fallen victim to crimes or scams >

Hxxx also declared that they only flagged transactions as suspicious if the amount was over the daily limit of AUD 50,000. But once Selina provided evidence that she had actually attempted to do a transaction of AUD 51,000 and this was still not flagged, Hxxx changed to saying that sending a transaction of AUD 51,000 overseas was not regarded as suspicious.

Regulator F was in favour of Hxxx, based on the reason that Regulator F does not have power to look into AML-related areas. Nevertheless, Hxxx bank proposed giving Selina AUD 2,500 if she agreed to close all her disputes against them. Selina had rejected it.

Eventually, the Ombudsman of Regulator F decided that the bank should compensate Selina AUD 2,000 for stress and inconvenience caused by the bank's delays in recalling the fund and its failure in complying with its investigation obligation. Meanwhile, this reserved Selina's right to continue to pursue legal actions against Hxxx for areas that are outside the power of Regulator F; that is, AML-related areas, such as why can AUD 49,600 (above AUD 10,000) be sent out of Australia in a single day and in a single transaction without any flagging or alerting, and why can AUD 118,000 be initialized by a civilian to leave Australia in only 14 days without flagging or alerting?

When compensating AUD 2,000, Hxxx attempted to remove Selina's rights by asking her to sign a deed with an additional clause to stop all her legal actions in the whole matter. Hxxx also attempted to keep Selina silent by adding a clause not to disclose this matter to anybody. Selina immediately rejected the deed and reported to Regulator F about Hxxx's attempt to add additional clauses on top of Regulator F's determination.

Eventually, Selina received AUD 2,000 without signing the deed.

Selina also contacted regulator AUSTRAC, who is responsible for determining whether a bank has violated AML or not. After a few discussions, AUSTRAC decided to use her information for their specialist team for investigation against Hxxx.

However, current regulations generally prohibit AUSTRAC from informing Selina, other banking regulators or tribunals on the final outcome of their investigation against a bank. And AUSTRAC is not the regulator deciding the compensation a bank must pay to customers.

With Regulator F having no power to look at the relevant areas, and AUSTRAC having the power to decide but not being allowed to disclose the outcome to any court, it seems hard for individuals to pursue compensation if their banks have broken the law.

Selina has reserved the right to continue to sue Hxxx.

* The above is not to criticise the handling of any regulator, but to record facts that happened in Selina's attempts to sue a bank for your understanding.

* Apparently, the above situation does not only occur in Australia, but also in many other developed countries.

Later, a government officer suggested that Selina may be able to apply under the FOI (Freedom of Information) Act. FOI gives the public the right to access AUSTRAC documents, provided those documents are not exempt from public release under the Act. In Selina's case, she applied for information in relation to herself (to see if any bank had logged suspicious reports against her) and on Hxxx's AML/CTF rules.

However, AUSTRAC rejected Selina's request regarding Hxxx documents twice, stating that those documents are exempt from public release under the Act. A government officer suggested Selina either seek an external review of the FOI request, or hire a lawyer to ask the court to order Hxxx bank to release their AML/CTR rules. However, as discussed in chapter 11 of this book, lawyers are generally not knowledgeable on AML/CTR rules.

Now, an external review of the FOI request may be Selina's last hope.

Ixxx bank

... attempted to convince the Singapore banking regulator that there was no sign their bank account was illegitimate by providing a "Suspicious Transaction Report (STR)" against "the transaction" (possibly referring to Selina's transaction). That STR showed that there was no basis to say that "the transaction" (possibly referring to Selina's transaction) was suspicious.

But Selina found that the STR that Ixxx sent to regulator was outdated—generated a few months before Singapore Interpol took over the case. Selina immediately informed the regulator.

Further, Ixxx bank used Hxxx's delay (1.5 months) in requesting them to chase the fund as the reason not to compensate.

Later, Ixxx argued that the regulator does not have the power to look into this specific case. Now, Selina's only option is to bring the case to court.

Singapore courts require plaintiffs to attend meetings in person in Singapore at least twice throughout the process, which may take years, as warned by a lawyer. Selina suspects that it may be more cost-effective for her to recover her money by concentrating on work than to continue to sue Ixxx, which requires her to keep flying to Singapore and engaging lawyers.

Selina has not made a final decision.

Jason

Selina sees Jason again as a result of her being a romance scam IT detective. The prior prophecy six years ago deemed to be spoken by the Holy Spirit (Chapter 2) that Selina would see Jason again in three to nine years yields.

After three years of "marriage" with the teenager, Jason rapidly started looking very old and unhealthy. Interestingly, the teenager also seemed to have aged significantly, looking more like a 30- or 40-year-old woman. Selina could barely see that she was the "teenager". As expected, however, Jason insisted with a sick and vague voice that he had a decent marriage—as victims normally say ... before their alleged partners finally receive permanent migration visas.

When Selina went back home, she thought of Jason looking so old and sick and burst into tears. She blamed herself for her failure to save Jason from harm, her failure in preventing him from entering into such a contract three years ago.

It was also found that Jason had been conned into changing his own official residential address in the government record. With different residential addresses, Jason and the teenager were considered officially separated for half a year, though Jason did not seem to be aware of this at all. Anecdotally, a person can divorce her partner after a year's separation, and still possibly get more than 50% of the marital house. (Please note, this is based on a friend's experience and Internet information. We are IT consultants, not legal consultants. This statement may be subject to inaccuracy.)

*Selina presented additional findings and several ridiculous problems about this girl to Jason and other stakeholders. (Not all major problems were listed in this book.) The pastor **wanted to believe** that every individual enters marriage for genuine reasons, ignoring all the **very red flags and on-going major issues**. After all, the teenager had built a relationship with this pastor and the church for three years. The pastor blamed Selina for bringing up these issues, especially since he was a host for the church where the "wedding" was held. But Selina asked herself, 'I have saved so many people around the world. Why should I only not save Jason, only because he is the love of my life???'*

* The above is not to criticise the church. Pastors are human. (Refer to the Bible and human history.) It is to illustrate typical responses by friends of alleged victims in similar cases.

Perhaps Selina should thank Frederick. Experiencing the crime, Selina's understanding of the psychology and tricks in romance scams was vastly enhanced. After all, Selina was not only a victim, but had also become a romance scammer (against criminals)! Selina became much more certain about the teenager's problems and was dedicated to informing Jason about the harm he was facing. Selina became confident enough to present her findings to Jason and other stakeholders, and from there, even more major problems with the teenager were discovered.

The crime did not destroy Selina, but gave her a stronger heart, richer knowledge and stronger technical skills to help herself and other people.

I'm Selina Co,
Romance Scam
IT Detective.

Not because I
choose to be,
now...

because
I have to be.

INTERESTING FACTS ABOUT
ROMANCE SCAMS

✓ Most victims have higher education levels and possibly higher IQ than their fraudsters.

Lying and acting are the key skills for romance scammers / marriage fraudsters. Fake male lovers behave like polite, considerate and nice gentlemen; fake female lovers behave like innocent, nice and helpless ladies.

✓ Many victims do not realize themselves are victimized after spending 2-3 years with the fake lovers. Indeed, the longer they are in the "relationship", the harder for them to realize (or accept) themselves have been victimized.

✓ Internet romance scams generally have no relation to hackers or IT professionals.

Many people misunderstand that Internet romance scammers are strong IT people—it is untrue. They only know a little bit more than victims **in very relevant areas**. In general, their IT skills are quite fair. (Refer to later chapters of this book.)

However, if you use the Internet in an insecure way, whoever can hack you easily. Please exercise security measures such as:

i) Always use complex password, with mix of at least numbers, uppercase and lowercase letters using non-dictionary words and non-names.

ii) Do not open suspicious files.

iii) Always have anti-virus software installed in your PC.

iv) When connected to public WiFi, especially hotel WiFi, avoid accessing bank accounts or any sensitive personal data.

✓ Male, female and gender X can all fall victim in romance scams.

✓ Victims can be as young as under 18. Please refer to government statistics.

✓ Many beautiful female Internet lovers are acted by male fraudsters (by occasionally playing tapes of female voices and daily texting through Internet applications).

✓ Some romance scam victims have already bought wedding dresses when they eventually find that the online lover have never existed.

✓ Romance scammers only leave victims when:

i) Their purposes have been achieved: victims are completely bankrupt and under heavy loans for the scam; and / or fraudsters receive permanent marriage visas (for marriage fraud).

Typically, the process takes few years.

ii) They cannot think of more excuses for money.

iii) Victims found that these may be or are surely scams. Victims block fraudsters.

iv) Victims found they are fraudsters and "kindly" inform fraudsters (which help fraudsters improve their scams. They will surely do better on their next victims after your kind feedback.)

✓ While majority of romance scam victims are in love with the fake people, some have never actually fallen in love. According to victims' interview in news, these victims only feel angry and insulted, instead of heartbroken.

✓ Some fall victim because of greed: hollow promises of "no need to work" after marrying the fake person, guaranteed permanent residence in the United States—you can see all these tricks in this book.

Similarly, some fall victim because they are too kind and too sincere: they believe fraudsters' stories of medical needs, children or parents' needs or business crisis.

Finally, some fall victim because they are too much of a gentleman, buying gifts or paying cash to online female lovers who had never existed and often role-played by male fraudsters.

✓ Typical romance scam / marriage fraud victims encounter psychological and emotional trauma. Victims often go through stages of grief similar to those who have lost a loved one in death. (Quote from *Brett M. Christensen - https://www.hoax-slayer.net/victims-dating-scams-psychological-emotional-trauma/*)

Victims can experience extreme anger, feelings of grief and loss, and often, intense feelings of shame. They may also experience a generalised loss of trust in others, and sometimes withdrawal and isolation.

Even Selina had never fallen in love with the fake person, she did encounter the above for few days.

✓ Victims also feel the lack of understanding and support from the wider community as well as friends and family.

Individuals in the community generally do not understand why people are falling victims in romance scams and marriage fraud, before themselves are victimized. Will you say, 'Government warns that there are romance scams. I think I may fall victim one day'? Instead, most people say, 'Government warns that there are romance scams. It cannot possibly happen to me. How will people lose their life savings to someone that they only met online (romance scams)? Or how will people trust wives who have never loved them (marriage fraud)?

✓ Many people thought romance scams only target middle-aged and older people—it is wrong. However, it is true that romance scams have much bigger impact on older victims than younger ones because:

    i) Younger victims do not have much life savings to lose, while older victims' life savings are all or almost all they have.

    ii) Older victims, especially those approaches retirement age, can barely gain back the money by working;

    iii) Younger victims have too many attractions when everyone around is single. Therefore, they may walk away from a romance relation more easily, no matter if it is fake or genuine.

✓ It is said that some victims are unwilling to believe these are scams even if you can show them evidences. I believe there are two reasons:

    i) they do not fully understand those evidences, or

    ii) there is "something" attached. Take chapters 5 and 6 as examples, even Selina was only victimized for 3 months and had never actually fallen "in love" with the fake person, when Selina noticed she was victimized, she found it very hard to believe. It took her about 2 weeks to fully detach the feeling (Chapter 7) when solid evidences are all in front of her.

Can be much worse for those who have actually fallen in love with the fake lovers for years.

✓ There have been known reports that very few victims, definitely not all, continue to send money even they somehow know their Internet lovers are fake. These are their addictions to the fancy worlds created by liars. These rare victims are unwilling to leave the beautiful dreams.

✓ Some individuals' faces are frequently stolen by romance scammers to create thousands of fake dating profiles. I guess it is because those African scammers cannot tell what Caucasian or Asian faces are considered to be "good-looking". Therefore, they keep using same faces which have been producing "good results".

However, these days, more scammers are using different people's faces randomly.

✓ There has been a slogan about romance scams, "If it is too good to be true, then it probably is". While this slogan protects many people, it also misleads others who consider themselves to be good-looking and wealthy. Like Selina's case, Selina did not consider Frederick "too good to be true".

It may also explain why some successful, wealthy individuals lose millions of dollars to scammers—the fake online lovers do not look "too good to be true" to them.

✓ According to news, individuals whose faces are "popularly" stolen by scammers say that they get contacted by new victims from around the world every week. These female victims say they are deeply in love with them and, in some cases, have emptied their bank accounts for them.

Take Bryan Denny as an example, the real him is a happily married family man. But his image has been stolen and used thousands of times in fake Facebook, Instagram and online dating profiles.

✓ Some victims, after they find they were scammed, are eager to find the actual owner of the stolen photos used by their scammers. Even though some victims rationally know the owners of the photos are not the same people they had "built relationship" with, they still want to be in love with the owners of the photos. As mentioned, there is "something" attached in a romance scam.

Unfortunately, owners of the stolen photos are often unwilling to be contacted by victims.

✓ According to police, many romance scam victims encounter break down in relationships with their own friends and families. Some, but not all, romance scammers intentionally isolate victims from their families and friends because:

i) families and friends can be those who are likely to warn victims of the scam.

ii) when victims no longer have trusted friends and families around, the fake online lovers' position in victims' hearts rise. Then they can lure victims more easily.

Furthermore, it is reported that families and friends who tried repeatedly to warn their loved ones about possible scams can feel angry and betrayed by victims for not being believed or trusted. Family members may also feel victims giving large sums of money to strangers have refused to listen to their warnings. Loved ones feel a sense of betrayal that victims put strangers before themselves. (Quote from *Brett M. Christensen*)

Once the scam has been finally realised, victims feel a sense of shame in front of their families and friends.

✓ Some clever victims are not warned by their friends and colleagues even after hearing the stories, because they believe the clever ones must have done correct judgement.

(Selina had told a successful entrepreneur about Frederick; but he also didn't notice it was a scam because he trusted Selina was usually considered to be clever.)

✓ The general public, at least friends and strangers that I have talked to, do not know money cannot be recovered by catching the scammer. Not knowing the risk makes potential victims less careful in deciding to send out their money.

✓ It is believed that 70%-90% of romance scams have gone unreported, according to government authorities.

You may also have a best friend or two who have lost a fortune in romance scams, but they haven't told you.

✓ Some government authorities use financial data to identify romance scam victims. And, in most identified cases, they indeed are.

✓ Some (not many) victims lose their job as a result of the crime, possibly because scammers immerse them into beautiful dreams of "no need to work after marrying him" or "you will become the wife of a boss of an enterprise soon". Victims become less dedicated in working and end up losing their jobs.

✓ It is not uncommon to see people lose over $100,000, according to authorities. Some lose over a million.

✓ While it is generally believed that Nigeria and Ghana are accountable for most Internet romance scams, there are reports on romance scammers in South Africa, the Philippines, Russia, South America and others.

There are also members of romance scams criminal groups who reside in most developed countries. However, reasonably, the heavier the penalty in a country, the less people in that country will commit the crime.

ROMANCE SCAMS VS MARRIAGE FRAUD

Before we start, there are few terminologies that look similar and the definitions varies by jurisdiction. Here is what we are referring to in this book:

1) **A fake marriage or sham marriage** refers to a marriage of convenience entered into, where both parties have no intention to create a real marital relationship.

   An example is the lady in Selina's church who paid the guy to pretend de-facto with her, in order for her to get a permanency residency in Australia (Chapter 2).

   It is illegal in most jurisdiction. Citizen of the country can be sentenced to jail. I do personally know someone sentenced to jail for this crime …

2) **Marriage fraud** is a type of romance scam, in which one spouse is unwittingly taken advantage of by the foreign spouse who feigns romantic interest, typically in order to obtain a country's residency or for money.

   An example is the friend of Cantonese man that Selina met in the barbeque, who is a victim of marriage fraud (Chapter 2).

   P.S. In the United states and some other countries, "marriage fraud" generally refers to both marriage fraud (one party defrauds another person who believes that their marriage is genuine) and fake marriage (both parties know the marriage does not intend to be genuine marriage, but only for monetary or residency benefits).

To differentiate it, this book refers marriage fraud only as one spouse defrauds another person who believes that their marriage is genuine.)

3) **Married but not for love** happens when both parties willingly stay in a marriage not because of love. It happens when one party want to get long term sexual benefit or for political reasons, while the other party want to gain financial benefit or social status from the marriage.

   Both parties somehow know the intention of each other. This type of marriage can last permanently, or until one of the parties can no longer give the agreed benefit to another party. For example, the wealthy husband is no longer wealthy and can no longer provide financial or social status benefits.

4) **Marriage that does not work** out refers to genuinely attempted to contribute to a marriage, which eventually fails due to various reasons.

   From the above, 1), 3) and 4) have both parties knowing true intentions of each other. Only 2) **marriage fraud** has one party fake the romantic interest to get his / her victim into a marriage, and the other party (the victim) does not know the romance is fake.

Marriage fraud is a type of romance scam. They share many similarities and have few differences:

• Both are related to marriage.

  In almost all (if not all) Internet romance scams, scammers immerse victims into beautiful pictures of their future marriage with the fake person;

  In marriage fraud, fraudsters immerse victims into beautiful pictures of their marriage.

- Both are based on lies and acting.

  Whenever you ask him / her, he / she will say, 'Yes, of course I love you.' 'I would rather die than to lose you!', etc. He/she will do something to prove his /her love. (eg. In romance scams, he /she may send you gifts to prove the "love"; In marriage fraud, she may have sex to "prove" the love.)

  However, liars are always only liars. No matter how good they act, there must be some small things that tell you they have never been genuine.

- Both are based on hollow promises. Victims are fully committed to the liars, but the liars fake their commitments to victims.

  In both marriage fraud and romance scams, fraudsters promise to stay with the victim forever but have never actually intended.

- Both are based on relationship and escalated with time.

  In romance scams, a scammer talks to a victim day and night. They build relation, they talk about a beautiful future together and even plans to have children. The fraudster will only raise illegitimate requests after he/she finds the victim get used to this "relationship". How can the victim believe someone he/she has talked day and night for months or years has never been real?

  Just as in marriage fraud, a fraudster stays with a victim day and night. Some even occasionally have sex. The fraudster and the victim build relation, build trust, with the fraudster. How can the victim believe someone they have been staying with day and night for years have never been genuine?

  However, only genuine people are genuine. For marriage fraudsters and romance scammers, no matter how well the act and lies, there must be a number of small things that looks wrong.

- Both take few years, unless you discover it earlier and leave.

  For romance scams, it is usual to see victims fallen in Internet romance scams for 2-3 years;

  For marriage fraud, in most known cases, fraudsters stay with victims for 4 to 8 years.

  Most marriage fraudsters will eventually tell victims the truth and leave soon after they get permanent residency; but some fraudsters who are ambitious to get victims' wealth may stay a few years longer.

- Both marriage fraudsters and romance scammers make you invest vastly in them, financially and emotionally. Once again, like gambling psychology that we explained earlier, the more efforts and money you put into the relationship, the more you become reluctant to accept they are fake.

  But no matter how much effort you invest, fake people will never become real.

- Unfortunately, the more the victim invested in the fake relation, the stronger the emotional breakdown will be when it is finally found to be fraud.

- In later stage, romance scams and marriage fraud are often mixed with both psychology torture and romance. What does psychology torture here refer to?

  To understand it, here is a solid example in the Bible. *Judges: 16: 15-17:*

  > *Then she said to him (Samson), 'How can you say, 'I love you,' when you won't confide in me? This is the third time you have made a fool of me and haven't told me the secret of your great strength.' With such nagging she prodded him day after day until he was sick to death of it.*

  > *So he told her everything …*

(background of the story: the woman would receive hundred shekels of silver if she successfully lure Samson into showing her his secret. Samson, the victim, died as a result.)

On the one hand, he /she tells you 'I love you most! You are my everything!'; but at the same time, he/she lures you into what he/she wants.

Some fraudsters also blackmail to end the relation if victims refuse to do what they want. Yet, blackmail does not always happen.

- Marriage fraud victims are not quite protected by law, to my knowledge. Even if there are sufficient evidences that the woman has left the victim soon after getting permanent residence, it is still not possible to void the marriage under the laws of many developed countries. The harm done can hardly be reversed. Best is to prevent.

  Internet romance scam victims are, in principle, protected by law. But practically, they are also not quite protected by law if the crime involves foreign countries because they are in different legislation (See explanation in later chapters of this book). It is also because Internet crime are relatively complex and require a lot of resources and international cooperation to crack.

  Other real-life or Internet romance scam victims are generally more protected if all involved parties are in the same country.

- Friends are more likely to warn you about romance scams than marriage fraud. It is because people generally believe in marriage and cannot accept marriage fraud can happen to themselves or their friends.

  But it is also true that romance scams do happen more frequently than marriage fraud. It is because anyone from anywhere in the world can use Internet (and real life) in attempt to commit a romance scam; while only people who physically reach you can attempt to commit marriage fraud against you.

Furthermore, a romance scammer can scam many people at the same time; but a marriage fraudster can only commit marriage fraud against one person at a time.

Finally, romance scammers can get one's money in only few months. In contrast, marriage fraud normally takes years to achieve fraudster's purposes.

- Public's attitude towards victims:

  In marriage fraud, marriages did officially exist. Some of the public have little sympathy towards marriage fraud victims because most victims (especially male) did get sexual benefits from the "relation". It is also because people generally believe marriage is complex and try not to comment.

  In romance scams, scammers only promise marriages, which never actually come true. Victims indeed get no benefits at all and the public generally have some sympathy towards them.

- In Internet romance scams, no matter how much efforts victims pay, the fake relation will never come true. Because, the fake online lovers have never ever existed.

  In marriage frauds, no matter how much efforts victims pay, the fake relation will also never come true. Because fraudsters who commit these are cold blooded.

UNWILLINGNESS
TO SEEK HELP

Potential victims of romance scams are usually unwilling to seek help. Firstly, they sincerely trust their romance scammers. It may not even be because they are in love, but humans trust other people based on their interactions. Romance scam victims are **talking to and building relationship with fraudsters day and night for months or years**— look realistic. How can they imagine they have been scammed?

Secondly, as mentioned, using "signs" or "red flags" to identify romance scams **lack reliable evidence**. "Signs" and "red flags" only mean the lovers are "likely" to be fake, but uncertain. And, don't forget scammers can provide fake evidence (such as fake company websites, fake passports, fake banking documents, fake LinkedIn profiles, fake third-party witnesses) to support their stories.

Finally, the public wrongly believes that only stupid people would fall victims in romance scams. Victims and potential victims **feel embarrassed** even to question whether they have been scammed or not.

As you can see in the examples in Chapter 13, many victims are very clever and highly educated. Professors, successful business persons, IT consultants—all can fall victim. There is nothing to be ashamed about falling victim.

Clever or stupid

Some people pride themselves on successfully identifying Internet romance scammers. In fact, in most cases, it is not because they are clever, but only because their scammers are careless or unskilful. Another main reason why some people don't fall victim is because they are just not keen on the fake person the scammer was pretending to be.

In the past, Internet romance scam layouts used to be very simple ... not anymore. These days, Internet scams can be very sophisticated and highly confusing. You do not need to be stupid to fall victim. And you don't need to be proud if you don't.

POSTSCRIPT

Real or fake; good or bad

As you can see from the story, when I first found
I had fallen victim and lost 70% of my life savings,
I was mad, screaming at night.

But, since then, I have become less money-minded and
less frugal with myself and my family: I spent so much effort
in saving money for what? My money can all just disappear,
for a lie. Why not just spend it on my loved ones
and myself?

As a financial IT consultant and a new immigrant
who struggled to survive in earlier days, I had been strict
about spending money. I'm especially sorry that I was too
frugal towards my parents and my old uncles and aunts who
have been so loving to me. Since I'd left Macau years ago,
I forgot they were old. They used to take care of me, support
me a lot, but now they are going to retire and I actually
forgot this. It should have been time for me to take care
of and support them.

Next time, when we have a family gathering, I should be more generous at the family dinner and with gifts.

* * *

Going back to romance scams or other new crimes, sometimes we have to accept there are unfortunate happenings—like Internet romance scams, which are relatively new since 2005. Governments, legislation, international organizations, cybercrime law has been improving. But yet I am personally under an impression that criminals are improving their scams faster than governments and organizations' works to combat the crime.

I write this book to let the public have an idea about how IT analysis, current legislation, international relation, etc, can impact the existence of romance scam and victims.

I am hoping that this book will bring revolutionary solutions to romance scams. I may not be able to help myself, but I hope what I have done can help rooting out the crime.

Acknowledgement

Thanks to all the characters involved in this book (except the scammer Frederick Chong). If you are a character in this book, you probably can identify yourself, though I have used fake names for almost all characters, including myself.

Thanks to all my friends, and new friends, who have supported me since this incident.

Before specifically talking about this book, I would like to take the chance to give thanks to ACCC, who has been trying to help prevent different types of scams, including romance scams. Thanks also to all the organizations, campaigners, police forces and government authorities internationally who have been devoted to the fight against romance and other types of scams. Thanks to Meetup.com for their concern regarding my incident and similar ones.

Thanks to Australian Self-Publishing Group, for publishing this book, and helping me at each stage. And definitely, thanks for putting up with me, as I am a computer engineer, a brand new writer who did not understand the steps in publishing, and you consistently supported me.

Front cover was designed by myself, with the help of many friends, new friends and ASPG who gave me comments and tips on the front cover. A few graphic designers had attempted to do the front cover for me, but it ended up I still have chosen my own work as I am a picky artist.

Thanks to Australian Self-Publishing Group again, for the internal design of the book. Australian Self-Publishing Group did a very professional job on this. Fonts and some artworks are my own design, enhanced to industry standard by Australian Self-Publishing Group.

Thanks to my editor Elite Editing. This book is challenging—50% is rational IT analysis and reporting of legal issues in romance scams, but the other 50% is a fiction-like true story, with a spectrum of very different emotions and problems happening in society and human psychology. I think Elite Editing has done a great work.

Thanks to legal advices from Australian Copyright Council & Arts Law Centre of Australia. Pre-publication by Mark O'Brien Legal.

Thanks to friends who have given me comments on the writing, especially the white hat hackers, classmates in Andrew's marketing class and new friends in a camping event.

Acknowledgement to *Brett M. Christensen - https://www.hoax-slayer.net/victims-dating-scams-psychological-emotional-trauma/*) contributed to two points in "Appendix 1 – Interesting facts about Romance scams".

Photo credits: thanks to all the actual people in the photos. In addition to that:

Photo A, Video 1 & 2: Acknowledgement to Francis.

Photo E, G: Likely to be created by criminals, unfortunately.

Photo F: Acknowledgement to Jason.

Photo K: Copyright owner unknown. (Sent from criminal to Selina)

Photo L: Copyright owner unknown. (Sent from criminal to Selina)

Photo M: Copyright owner unknown. (Sent from criminal to Selina)

Photo N: Thanks to Patrick Furlong from Santiago and his work, "A Bolivian man with his Alpaca (herd in background)" *https:// commons.wikimedia.org/wiki/File:Bolivian_Alpaca.jpg*

Photo O: Copyright owner unknown for the pair of familiar alpaca faces.

I used computer graphics to move the alpacas to Bondi beach. Bondi beach photo was taken by myself on Christmas Day 2018.

LOL picture in Chapter 9 was my own hand drawing. Figure 1, 2 & 3 were my own works.

Bride, queen and ring in Chapter 9 were my drawings to represent icons in Whatsapp with criminal, due to copyright reason. Flower and lightning in Chapter 4 were my drawings.

Thanks to Chris Medina for the song "What are Words".

Thanks to *Batman Forever—'I'm … Batman. Not because I have to be. Now … because I choose to be.'* (See the last black page of this book.)

Finally, thanks to alpacas. Thanks to the "Grass Mud Horse" …

Clarification

1. In Chapter 4, the scammer was unable to do a real-time video call with Selina. However, in recent days, there have been multiple reports that scammers can fake short, irresponsive real-time video calls with their victims by playing video tapes.

2. In Chapter 4, Selina thought that the police would take time to identify whether it was a scam or not; but later when Selina showed Andy Frederick's passport, he could tell in a few seconds that it was fake.

    However, it can depend on the quality of the fake passport.

3. In Chapter 10, Selina encountered good people in a hackers' meeting. However, not all hackers' meetings are for white hat hackers. You may also encounter bad people in a hackers' meeting.

www.ingramcontent.com/pod-product-compliance
Lightning Source LLC
Chambersburg PA
CBHW071111050326
40690CB00008B/1189